CFA Institute Conference Proceedings

Points of Inflection: New Directions for Portfolio Management

Proceedings of the AIMR seminar "Points of Inflection: New Directions for Portfolio Management"

26–27 February 2004
New York City

CFA Institute would like to thank the following for their time and contribution to the conference:

Robert D. Arnott, *moderator*
Peter L. Bernstein
Richard M. Ennis, CFA
Gary L. Gastineau
Paul R. Greenwood, CFA
Martin L. Leibowitz
Paul McCulley
André F. Perold
Jeremy J. Siegel
Laurence B. Siegel
Fred H. Speece, Jr., CFA, *co-moderator*
M. Barton Waring

GUIDING PURPOSE | The CFA Institute Conference Proceedings series publishes current and highly relevant ideas and research presented at various CFA Institute Conferences. Articles are written in a precise, easy-to-read, and accurate manner that is consistent with the intent and spirit of the original presentation. In so doing, the Conference Proceedings Series advances the CFA Institute mission to lead the investment profession globally by setting the highest standards of education, integrity, and professional excellence.

CFA INSTITUTE CONFERENCE PROCEEDINGS
(USPS 013-739 ISSN 1535-0207) 2004

ISBN 1-932495-18-5
2004, no. 4
Printed in the United States of America
14 July 2004

This publication is designed to provide accurate and authoritative information with regard to the subject matter covered. It is sold with the understanding that the publisher is not engaged in rendering legal, accounting, or other professional services. If legal advice or other expert assistance is required, the services of a competent professional should be sought.

Copies are mailed as a benefit of membership to CFA® charterholders. Subscriptions also are available at $100.00 USA. For one year. Address all circulation communications to CFA Institute Conference Proceedings, 560 Ray C. Hunt Drive, Charlottesville, Virginia 22903, USA; Phone 434-951-5499; Fax 434-951-5262. For change of address. Send mailing label and new address six weeks in advance.

Is published six times a year in March, March, May, August, September, and September, by CFA Institute at 560 Ray C. Hunt Drive, Charlottesville, VA. **Periodical postage paid at Charlottesville, Virginia, and additional mailing offices.**

Postmaster: Please send address changes to CFA Institute Conference Proceedings, CFA Institute, P.O. Box 3668, Charlottesville, Virginia 22903.

Contents

This proceedings qualifies for credit under the guidelines of the Professional Development Program. Using Reference Time, this proceedings qualifies for 4 credit hours. The self-test for this proceedings can be found at www.cfainstitute.org/pdprogram/self-tests_list.html. For more information on the PD Program (including how to use Clock Time and the Standard Documentation in lieu of the self-test), go to www.cfainstitute.org/pdprogram.

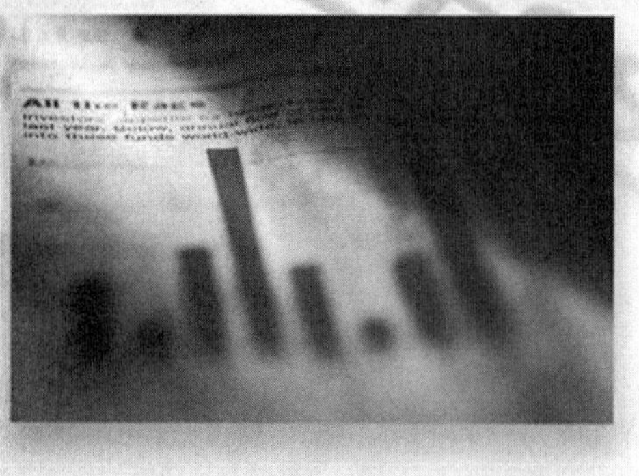

Focus On

Equity

The following is a sample of the wealth of information on Equity found in the Education Central area of the CFA Institute website:

Featured Publications

www.cfa**pubs**.org

Equity Analysis Issues, Lessons, and Techniques
Conference Proceedings
(2004)

Equity Valuation in a Global Context
Conference Proceedings
(2004)

Value at Risk and Expected Stock Returns
Turan G. Bali and Nusret Cakici
(*Financial Analysts Journal*, March/April 2004)

Investing in Emerging Markets
Robert F. Bruner, Robert M. Conroy, CFA, Wei Li, Elizabeth F. O'Halloran, and Miguel Palacios Lieras
(*Research Foundation of AIMR Monograph*, 2003)

Global Evidence on the Equity Risk Premium
Elroy Dimson, Paul Marsh, and Mike Staunton
Summarized by Jonathan Hubbard, CFA
(*The CFA Digest*, May 2004)

Featured Webcasts

www.cfa**direct**.org

Global Politics Strikes Again?
Marvin Zonis
(May 2004)

Featured Conferences

www.cfainstitute.org/conferences

New Dimensions in Private Equity
13 October 2004
Chicago, IL, USA

Equity Research and Valuation Techniques
1–2 December 2004
Philadelphia, PA, USA

Authors

We would like to thank Robert Arnott for serving as moderator and Fred Speece for serving as co-moderator at this conference. Our thanks also go out to Peter Bernstein for writing the overview for this proceedings. Finally, we wish to express our sincere gratitude to the authors listed below for their contributions to both the conference and this proceedings:

Robert D. Arnott is chairman of Research Affiliates, LLC, as well as editor of the *Financial Analysts Journal*. He is also a visiting professor at the University of California at Los Angeles. Previously, Mr. Arnott was chairman at First Quadrant, LP. Mr. Arnott has served as a member of the editorial boards of the *Journal of Portfolio Management* and *Investment Policy* magazine, as a member of the Chairman's Advisory Council of the Chicago Board Options Exchange, and as a member of the product advisory boards of the Chicago Mercantile Exchange and Toronto Stock Exchange. He is the author of numerous articles and a four-time recipient of a Graham and Dodd Scroll, which is awarded by the *Financial Analysts Journal*. Mr. Arnott holds degrees in economics, applied mathematics, and computer science from the University of California.

Peter L. Bernstein is president of Peter L. Bernstein, Inc., an economic consultancy to institutional investors and corporations. He also writes analyses of the capital markets and real economy for his firm's semimonthly publication *Economics & Portfolio Strategy*. Previously, Mr. Bernstein taught economics at Williams College and the New School and worked in commercial banking. He is the founding editor and, currently, a consulting editor of the *Journal of Portfolio Management*. Mr. Bernstein is the author of eight books and many articles, including *Against the Gods: The Incredible Story of Risk* and *Capital Ideas: The Improbable Origins of Modern Wall Street*. He is a recipient of the Graham and Dodd Award of Excellence, awarded by the *Financial Analysts Journal*, and the Award for Professional Excellence and the James R. Vertin Award, awarded by CFA Institute. Mr. Bernstein is a graduate of Harvard University.

Richard M. Ennis, CFA, is principal at Ennis, Knupp & Associates, where he consults with clients and directs the firm's investment policy research. Additionally, he is chairman of the board of directors. Previously, he was affiliated with A.G. Becker, O'Brien (now Wilshire) Associates and Transamerica Investment Management Company. Mr. Ennis is sought as an expert witness in fiduciary and investment litigation, and his research has been published in such journals as the *Financial Analysts Journal* and *Journal of Portfolio Management*. His real estate research received the *Financial Analysts Journal*'s Graham and Dodd Award of Excellence in 1991. Mr. Ennis holds a BS from California State University at Northridge and an MBA from the University of California at Los Angeles.

Gary L. Gastineau is a managing director of ETF Consultants, LLC, which provides specialized exchange-traded fund (ETF) consulting services to ETF issuers, exchanges, market makers, research organizations, and investors. Previously, he served as managing director of ETF product development at Nuveen Investments. Mr. Gastineau is the author of *The Exchange-Traded Funds Manual* and *The Options Manual* and co-author of the *Dictionary of Financial Risk Management* and *Equity Flex Options*. He is a recipient of the Bernstein Fabozzi/Jacobs Levy Award for an Outstanding Article for "Equity Index Funds Have Lost Their Way" (*Journal of Portfolio Management*). Mr. Gastineau serves on the editorial boards of the *Journal of Derivatives*, *Journal of Indexes*, and *Contemporary Finance Digest* and is a member of the Review Board of the Research Foundation of CFA Institute. He is an honors graduate of both Harvard College and Harvard Business School.

Martin L. Leibowitz is a managing director in the research department of Morgan Stanley. Previously, he served as vice chairman and chief investment officer at the Teachers Insurance and Annuity Association-College Retirement Equities Fund (TIAA-CREF), where he was responsible for the overall management of all TIAA-CREF investments. Dr. Leibowitz has authored several books and more than 130 articles, 9 of which have received the *Financial Analysts Journal*'s Graham and Dodd Award of Excellence. He is a recipient of the Nicholas Molodovsky Award and the James R. Vertin Award, awarded by CFA Institute. In 1995, he received the Distinguished Public Service Award from the Public Securities Association and became the first inductee into the Fixed Income Analysts Society's Hall of Fame. Dr. Leibowitz is a trustee of the Carnegie Corporation, the Institute for Advanced Study at Princeton, and the Research Foundation of CFA Institute. Dr. Leibowitz holds a BA and an MS from the University of Chicago and a PhD in mathematics from the Courant Institute of New York University.

Paul McCulley is a managing director and portfolio manager at Pacific Investment Management Company (PIMCO). Previously, Mr. McCulley served as an account manager and monetary policy specialist at PIMCO and as chief economist for the Americas at UBS Warburg. He holds a bachelor's degree from Grinnell College and an MBA from Columbia University Graduate School of Business.

Jeremy J. Siegel is Russell E. Palmer Professor of Finance at the Wharton School of the University of Pennsylvania. Additionally, he is the academic director of the U.S. Securities Industry Institute. Previously, Professor Siegel taught at the Graduate School of Business of the University of Chicago and served as head of economics training at JP Morgan & Company. He has appeared on CNN, CNBC, and "Wall $treet Week" and is the author of numerous professional articles and two books, including *Stocks for the Long Run*. Professor Siegel is a graduate of Columbia University and holds a PhD in economics from Massachusetts Institute of Technology.

Laurence B. Siegel is director of investment policy research at the Ford Foundation. Previously, he served as a managing director at Ibbotson Associates, an investment consulting firm that he helped establish in 1979. Mr. Siegel is the author of *Benchmarks and Investment Management*, an AIMR Research Foundation monograph. He chairs the investment committee of the Trust for Civil Society in Central and Eastern Europe and serves on the investment committee of the NAACP Legal Defense Fund. Mr. Siegel is also a member of the editorial board of the *Journal of Portfolio Management* and the research review board of the Research Foundation of CFA Institute. He holds a BA in urban studies and an MBA in finance from the University of Chicago.

M. Barton Waring is managing director and head of the Client Advisory Group at Barclays Global Investors, where he advises institutional investors on total portfolio and total asset class investment concerns. Previously, he served as head of Ibbotson Associates, as regional practice leader at Towers Perrin Asset Consulting, and as head of the defined-contribution business at Morgan Stanley Asset Management. Mr. Waring has written many articles on topical issues in finance and is a regular speaker at industry conferences. He holds a BS in economics from the University of Oregon, a JD from Lewis & Clark College, and an MBA in finance from Yale University.

Overview: A Fifth Point of Inflection

Peter L. Bernstein
President
Peter L. Bernstein, Inc.
New York City

At the 2003 AIMR (now called CFA Institute[1]) Annual Conference, I gave a presentation in which I discussed what I saw as four points of inflection in the investment management industry: the demise of soft-dollar research, the reduced role of indexing, the escape from benchmarking and with it a greater reliance on absolute returns, and the impending death of long-only as a conventional strategy.[2] Clearly, these points of inflection were the focus of the presentations at the February 2004 conference—"Points of Inflection: New Directions for Portfolio Management"—on which this proceedings is based.

The Four Points

The authors in this proceedings have taken the four points of inflection I proposed in 2003 and looked at them with their own critical eyes. **Paul McCulley** makes some very profound observations. He describes the U.S. political economy as an "uneasy marriage between democracy and capitalism" and then illustrates how history has shown where the inflection points occur between the oscillating dominance of the competing forces of democracy and capitalism.

Addressing the "point" of the long-only constraint, **Richard Ennis** relates how greater flexibility can be introduced into policy portfolios not only by eliminating the long-only constraint but also by using a comprehensive "master manager" approach that, in part, separates how investors earn the return of the policy portfolio (beta) from how they seek to exploit security mispricing (alpha). Similarly, **Laurence Siegel** sees portfolios as being composed of a beta component, which is broad asset class exposure, and an alpha component, which is excess return achieved through active management. He cautions that if investors are hiring active managers, presumably because they believe these managers have real skill or the ability to deliver alpha, then they ought to be sure that they are paying for true alpha and not beta. **Martin Leibowitz** expands further on the policy portfolio issue and uses investor behavior as evidence supporting the need for a more fluid, adaptive policy portfolio that is responsive to discernible changes in the market.

Robert Arnott examines the long-term return outlook (for both stocks and bonds) and finds that it is not a rosy one, nor is the outlook for the equity risk premium. But despite this grim outlook, he sees several ways for managers to improve returns. In the same vein as Arnott, **Jeremy Siegel** looks at the long-run equity risk premium. Siegel believes that based on various indicators, the future equity return outlook is not as grim as suggested by Arnott and still offers a reasonable risk premium over bonds.

Finally, **Barton Waring** discusses what he believes to be the characteristics of successful active managers of the future: They will have skill in forecasting alpha, optimize their portfolios on the active efficient frontier, be moving away from using the long-only constraint, and have high breadth, good portfolio construction processes, low transaction costs, and stringent risk controls. And **Gary Gastineau** picks up on the "point" of indexing and says that although indexing has problems, the problems are not insurmountable and can be remedied by doing such things as adopting silent indexes and, yes, even using elements of active-management strategies.

A Fifth Point

I am grateful for the deep thought that the authors in this proceedings have given to my original four points of inflection. I have been mulling over these points myself for the past year and see another important topic that I want to expand on that draws from the four points of inflection and that will ultimately lead me to a fifth point centered on the question: How efficient is the market? That is:

- Although there is a mass of empirical data suggesting market efficiency, is the market as efficient as it appears?
- Why is the market so hard to beat? Certainly, nobody thinks it is easy.
- Why do so many smart people chase one another's tails? Everybody is trying to get into the same act.

[1]Effective 9 May 2004, AIMR changed its name to CFA Institute.

[2]For a printed version of this talk, see Peter L. Bernstein, "Points of Inflection: Investment Management Tomorrow," *Financial Analysts Journal* (July/August 2003):18–23.

- Do we know what we are measuring when we say "beat the market"?
- How much active risk should active managers take?

These are big questions, and I will try to answer them. But my main conclusion is that the whole business is a lot more complicated than the studies of market efficiency, from Eugene Fama on up, would lead one to believe. I conclude, however, with a strong note of hope: There is gold in them thar hills that managers are not mining. But the interesting question is: If there is gold in the hills, why are managers not mining it?

The Open-End Format

I take my text for this sermon from a recent National Bureau of Economic Research working paper by Jeremy Stein of the Harvard economics department called "Why Are Most Funds Open-End? Competition and the Limits of Arbitrage."[3] This article is a must-read. Stein asks the basic questions: Why are most funds open-end, and why are most investment management contracts yearly? I will cite just a few words from Stein's article:

> The open-end form imposes serious constraints on would-be arbitrageurs. In particular, being open-end exposes arbitrageurs to the risk of large withdrawals if they perform poorly in the short run. This risk in turn makes it dangerous for them to put on trades that are attractive in a long-run sense, but where convergence to fundamentals is unlikely to be either smooth or rapid. (p. 2)

If the open-end format makes it so dangerous to put on trades where the convergence to fundamentals is unlikely to be either smooth or rapid, then why is the open-end format so prevalent? Almost all mutual funds are open-end, and almost all investment management contracts run no more than a year. Stein suggests that clients and shareholders are concerned that the managers they select will turn out to be either incompetent or dishonest and thus clients want to be able to get their money out if they are dissatisfied. Clients want to be sure that they have that option. So, mutual funds are open-end and contracts are short term. But is that the true reason that the open-end format is so widespread?

Stein says in this view the prevalence of open-end funds represents a socially efficient outcome because clients can get their money back if they are unhappy with performance or if they do not trust the manager. But he says this is not his view, and after reading his article, it is not my view either. He says the end result may be a degree of open-endedness that is socially excessive, and he then sets forth the following hypothesis: The gains for being able to undertake longer-horizon trades in a closed-end form should outweigh the potential losses that come from being unable to control wayward managers. That is, long-term contracts that involve locking up money may produce better overall returns, better results, even though clients cannot control a wayward manager.

Locking up money gives managers the opportunity to undertake longer-horizon trades, what Jack Treynor in a wonderfully simple expression once called "slow ideas." If managers can earn more significant alphas by making longer-term bets, then why does the investment management fraternity have such a hard time persuading people to let them manage money that way? If a manager went to one of his or her clients and said "we would like a five-year contract," what are the chances the client would say that is a great idea? None. The closed-end fund business is a tiny portion of the whole mutual fund area. People want the flexibility of the open-end.

Why the Open-End Format?

Why should it be that people want the open-end format? The answer, ladies and gentlemen, is that it is not those among you who are clients who are blocking the outcome of longer-term contracts but those among you who are managers. You are the ones who are blocking it. How can that be? Let me trace the process by using a thought exercise in an imaginary world where all investment management arrangements are closed-end. The client puts the money in and cannot get it back out for a given period of time, and for a closed-end mutual fund, that time is never—no withdrawals of funds under any circumstances; the funds are absolutely locked up. This is a world where nobody ever heard of open-end.

Among all these closed-end arrangements are a few managers who are really good and are making alphas like crazy. Imagine one of these firms in this closed-end arrangement with 10 successive years of statistically significant alpha. The firm's employees sit down to have a champagne lunch to celebrate this occasion, and the firm's president says: "Hey, we are passing up something. We are so good at this, and we are just managing this one limited pot of money. We should open it up and let more people bring money to us. It will be wonderful. We will have a tremendous inflow of money instead of this limited pot, and we will make lots of clients rich in the process. So, why are we sitting with this closed-end arrangement? Let's open this thing up."

[3]Jeremy C. Stein, "Why Are Most Funds Open-End? Competition and the Limits of Arbitrage," National Bureau of Economic Research Working Paper No. w10259 (issued in February 2004). This article can be found at www.ssrn.com.

Once one firm goes open-end, then everybody follows suit. The really good firms will be the first ones to open up because they know they will attract money. The slackers, the firms that cannot create alpha, will also have to go open-end because they would be identified as poor performers if they did not go open-end. The inevitable result is that asset gathering becomes the mark of success. And welcome to the world of today.

Consequences of the Open-End Format

In short, it is managers who open the funds up. And this result has major consequences for the way managers manage money and what happens to their clients. Managers have put themselves in the position of the sorcerer's apprentice, who thinks he has found a great form of magic but soon the magic is giving the commands instead of the apprentice. Those of us who manage money in open-end formats—either an open-end mutual fund or a one-year contract for management—are stuck with all kinds of problems. The open-end really has two ends: one where money comes in and the other where money goes out just as easily. As a result, managers are tied much more tightly to short-term strategies than they might like because they cannot persuade their clients to wait for the period of time that is required for a longer-term strategy to work out. Anybody who has managed money knows that feeling. Do you want to be underweight small cap when small cap is hot? Do you want to be overweight tech stocks when the bottom is falling out of tech stocks? Of course not. Contrarian strategies are very risky for managers, not only in terms of returns over the short run but also, more important, in terms of fickle clients or shareholders.

And it is not just managers who feel this kind of heat but also chief investment officers of institutions, foundations, endowment funds, and pension funds. They have to deal with investment committees and people higher up. If in any one year the Yale endowment fund is down 10 percent and the Harvard endowment fund is up 10 percent, David Swensen is going to be on the hot seat. In the January/February *Financial Analysts Journal*, Louis Chan and Josef Lakonishok say that value investing, or contrarian investing, earns a premium that is not due to higher risk in those kinds of companies, as Eugene Fama has suggested, but that is due to, and I quote, "behavioral considerations and the agency costs of delegated investment management" (p. 71).[4] This is what Stein is talking about: Managers are reluctant to take strong contrarian positions for fear that they will lose business, that funds will leave. Mark Kritzman wrote in *Economics & Portfolio Strategy* "even with perfect knowledge of expected return and distributions around them, annual volatility can be very wide if you make concentrated bets. And concentrated bets are where the big alphas reside."[5]

The fear of being wrong and alone is a very powerful one. Bill Miller, the miracle worker at Legg Mason, had compound returns of 28 percent a year from 1992 to 1999, but when the market turned down, he lost $1 billion; out went 12 percent of the assets under management, despite this proof that he had some kind of portfolio manager magic. Suppose Bill Miller had been able to go short in 1999 with the open-end format. How much money would he have lost? A pile of assets would have gone out before the year was over. If the focus is not on the short run in the management of money, why have mutual funds averaged 75 percent turnover for years, and even higher just recently? If the focus is not on the short run, why is minimizing trading costs so important? If a manager is turning over his or her portfolio almost once a year, then trading costs are enormously important and Plexus and other such firms are getting rich helping managers reduce their trading costs. If the focus is not on the short run, why are annual deviations from benchmark returns such an important element of client and consultant relations?

Hedge Funds. All of this adds up to some of the fascination with hedge funds, where in most cases withdrawals cannot be made on demand and money can be locked up. Why is that? The better hedge fund managers understand that asset gathering is poison to good performance, so they compensate that lockup with outrageous fees that make them happy with an asset pool that grows only as a matter of return. As I suggest later, this arrangement reveals what a more successful client/manager contract might look like.

Until recently, the predominant trend has been that investors put their money in open-end mutual funds because doing so allows them a high degree of flexibility. But as a result, they are getting suboptimal performance. I think that all of us in this business should begin to think more realistically and more systematically about the costs of liquidity in terms of lower returns versus the premium return that might be earned from locking clients' money up.

Or, maybe we should think about it the other way around: Alternative investments have reached

[4]Louis K.C. Chan and Josef Lakonishok, "Value and Growth Investing: Review and Update," *Financial Analysts Journal* (January/February 2004):71–86.

[5]*Economics & Portfolio Strategy* (New York: Peter L. Bernstein, Inc., 15 January 1998).

such a level of popularity that clients are willing to lock money up in less liquid investments, such as real estate and private equity. It is a new kind of arrangement, and investors are moving in this direction. The hedge fund phenomenon indicates that change is under way, and in time, this whole open-end model may shift. Thus, just as I suggested in my original points of inflection that long-only is a funny way to manage money when selling short is another opportunity, I am suggesting that using open-end formats and chasing short-term alphas is a "corset" on investment performance. If managers really want to try to earn alphas, statistically significant alphas, they have to have a broader horizon. The hedge fund business is an opportunity to try to take such a broader horizon. Not all hedge funds will do it well. There will be bad performance in the hedge fund area. But hedge funds have created for themselves an environment in which they can make decisions with much greater freedom than the conventional manager can, and that is the kind of environment that I would like to see on a much wider basis. Managers thus need to liberate themselves from the short-run pressures that exist if they fall behind in any one year. There are longer-term inefficiencies that managers are not exploiting because of the consequences of being wrong and alone in the short run.

Examples. Following are two specific examples of what I have been describing. First, the most successful investor of them all, the one we all hold up as the icon, Warren Buffett, sits happily behind the impregnable wall of a closed-end fund. You can trade Berkshire Hathaway all you want, but you cannot invade the company's assets. Second, unlike managers of open-end funds, managers of overpriced dot.com companies had no hesitation in betting against the Internet bubble. They sold shares to the public right when the market was going through the roof, the equivalent of going short during those giddy years. The public gobbled up their shares. It was an almost riskless proposition for them. If they were wrong, they could just sit on the cash. But again, it was a closed-end format. The dot.com companies sold shares, the money came in, and the shareholders may have felt bad about it but they could not raid the company and get the cash back; the closed-end format can take a big contrary bet.

Market Efficiency. With all this focus on the short term because of the fear of losing assets withdrawn by fickle clients, no wonder that mispricings and related aberrations in the market are short lived. No wonder the empirical evidence demonstrates that alphas are few and far between. No wonder that alphas are thin when they do exist. No wonder we find so much volatility around the mean alphas. Stephen Ross in a lecture a couple of years ago said there should be no doubt whatsoever over whether the efficiency glass is half-full or half-empty. It is simply quite full. No wonder the market is so efficient in the short run.

Happy Ending

But recognition of this short-term focus and short-term efficiency points to a happy ending that there is *hope*. Because of the open-end format, managers are not exploiting the mispricings that take longer to work out—Treynor's slow ideas. Consequently, the market may not be as efficient as the University of Chicago wants us to think it is. There is gold in them thar hills that we are not mining, and now we know why not.

The trend toward alternative investments and hedge funds shows that, on the client's side, views are beginning to shift. The notion of a lockup of funds is becoming a little bit more acceptable, as is the notion that it is fair enough to pay a higher fee because these managers resist the temptation to do asset gathering. Even absolute rather than relative performance is beginning to attract investors, which means liberation from the tyranny of benchmarks. So, some progress is being made toward a healthier format that is less short-term oriented and toward a greater opportunity to take risks, even over the long term—a fifth point of inflection. Welcome to the world of tomorrow.

When I think about the investment management business, I try to imagine what an investment contract with a five-year horizon, instead of a one-year horizon, would look like. I wonder how we can give the manager maximum leeway and still protect the client from incompetence and dishonesty. I do not have a final answer and have only begun to think about this problem, but perhaps one way to address the competence issue is to look at past performance. Past performance may not be a predictor of future performance, but it does say something about competence. In every study that I have seen, people who have a bad track record for five years are not about to start having a good track record. Somebody with a good track record can falter, but somebody with a bad track record does not work his or her way out of it. So, past experience does say something about competence. As far as dishonesty is concerned, even the open-end format does not prevent managers from stealing money from their clients. It offers no protection.

So, how about a five-year contract that the client signs, but the client can purchase options to quit at the end of any year, with the price of those options declining year by year? If a client wants to get out the first year, that option is very expensive. If the client wants to get out the third year, that option does not cost the client so much up-front. If the client wants to stay for the whole five years, the fee will be that much less.

So, I am talking about a five-year arrangement where if the client wants to get out sooner, it will cost the client. The idea is to give the manager the money for an extended period of time so that the manager is in a position to make longer-term bets than he or she could under the open-end format, where money can go out when the client chooses. That ability for money to come and go at will has to demand a price. If the client is willing to lock his or her money up for five years and does not buy the option, the fee is small.

My firm is not a law firm, and we do not manage any money, so I leave the details to others to work out. But I hope more investors have the opportunity to seek alpha where it may really reside and not only in short-run horizons. Seeking alpha over the long term, rather than the short term, would be a fifth point of inflection for our business, for our clients, for research, for everything that we do, and this new format would be much healthier for investors than our present format.

History Lessons for 21st Century Investment Managers

Paul McCulley
Managing Director and Portfolio Manager
Pacific Investment Management Company
Newport Beach, California

The United States can be thought of as a strained marriage of democracy and capitalism. That is, democracy and capitalism are often at odds with each other. History has shown where the inflection points occur between the dominance of democracy versus capitalism within the U.S. economy. Although managers should not assume that history will repeat itself in exactly the same fashion, it would be wise to use history as a guide in interpreting the secular changes presently occurring within the U.S. economy.

The U.S. national system can be described as a democratic, capitalist society. Most Americans assume that such a system is a good thing: We embrace both democracy and capitalism. But democracy and capitalism are inherently in conflict, and the conflict between the two is a source of major structural changes in the U.S. economy and secular trends in asset performance.

In this presentation, I will describe the nature of the uneasy marriage between democracy and capitalism, the mixed economy that results from this marriage, the ways in which the public sector of the economy dominated during the 1960s and 1970s, the reasons that domination ended, and the reasons that the private sector rose to dominance during the 1980s and 1990s. I will also discuss the ways in which I see the weight of dominance shifting back toward the public sector and what such a shift means for investment management in the future.

The Marriage of Democracy and Capitalism

Democracy is founded on a simple socialist principle—one person, one vote—which assures that each person (theoretically, at least) has equal influence in the system. Capitalism, in contrast, is founded on the principle of one dollar, one vote, which is known as a "cumulative voting system." The more dollars a person or voting entity has, the more votes that person has and, therefore, the more influence that person has in the system. This difference leads to an inherent conflict between these two coexisting systems—one that offers equal influence to each person and one that offers variable influence depending on wealth.

Winston Churchill once said that democracy and capitalism form the worst possible combination—except for all others. And he was right. Like all marriages, the one between democracy and capitalism is far from perfect, but it seems to work better than most, and the key variable that makes it work is the rule of law because within the rule of law is the ingredient that capitalism most requires—the sanctity of property rights. The gift of democracy to capitalism is property rights. Capitalism cannot function without property rights. And property rights cannot be guaranteed by a society that does not have a sense of equity and justice. Justice, however, cannot be guaranteed under the capitalist principle of cumulative voting because a voting system based on wealth implies that the wealthy can buy better justice, at which point justice loses its value along with property rights and the rule of law. Democracy—founded on the principle of one person, one vote—creates a framework in which all are afforded equal justice and no one is supposed to get the best justice that money can buy.

The system is like a delicately balanced seesaw: Democracy and capitalism sit at each end, teetering continuously up and down, and the rule of law and property rights act as the fulcrum in the middle.

Mixed Economy: Government and Capitalism. The U.S. economy and its markets is by nature a mixed economy. It consists of a public sector—call it "we-the-people," or government—and a private sector—call it "we-the-markets," or capitalism. Secular changes (or points of inflection) occur when we-the-people shift the weights in our economy. These shifting weights are manifested as either a bull market in we-the-people power or a bull market in we-the-markets power. One such secular change occurred in the 1979–81 period. Another such secular change is occurring right now and will have a tremendous effect on how investment professionals manage investments in the years ahead.

The 1979–81 secular change put an end to the bull market in government that had dominated the economy during the 1960s and 1970s. It ushered in the beginning of a bull market in capitalism that dominated the economy in the 1980s and 1990s. Thus, from 1979 to 1981, the invisible hand of the markets won out over the visible fist of the government. This bull market was the defining characteristic of the 1980s and 1990s, and it was hugely important because of a single conclusive variable—inflation. In the long sweep of history, bull markets in government have been shown to be inherently inflationary and bull markets in capitalism are inherently disinflationary. Thus, when an economy swings from one type of bull market to the other, the economy has reached a secular inflection point in inflation. Over the long run, the most important economic variable to get right is inflation. By understanding the status of inflation, investment managers can more effectively determine the relative valuation between tangible assets and financial assets and the various components within each of those categories. Thus, if investment managers can accurately assess which power is going to be in ascendancy—we-the-people or we-the-markets—then they are more likely to forecast inflation accurately. Many other strategic choices will naturally follow from that forecast.

President Carter's Cardigan Moment. The 1960s and 1970s constituted an inflationary period. It was a bull market in government and a bear market in capitalism. It ended because the bull market in government eventually created a lethal brew called "stagflation," which is the proximate reason that we-the-people, through the electoral process, decided to shift our weight toward a more market-based economy.

Some people believe that the bull market in government died on the day that Paul Volker became chairman of the U.S. Federal Reserve in August 1979. That is not a bad day to choose. I prefer to think that the change actually occurred on the evening in 1978 when President Jimmy Carter appeared on national television wearing a cardigan sweater and told us that we, the American people, were suffering from a malaise. Many people remember the malaise speech. Perhaps not as many people remember why he was wearing a cardigan sweater. The cardigan sweater was part of his energy program. At the time of the malaise speech, the United States did not have a capitalist energy sector. It had a government-controlled energy sector. It also had a serious energy shortage. And part of President Carter's solution for the shortage, which he recommended that evening to the American people, was to turn the thermostat down to 65 degrees and put on a sweater.

The American people responded with hearty disagreement. It was the beginning of a turn in the American psyche, an inflection point when the visible fist of government was about to be slapped aside by the invisible hand of the markets.

Good Things from the 1960s and 1970s. The 1960s and 1970s were a terrible time for financial assets. Stagflation is not a prescription for making lots of money on Wall Street. But the 1960s and 1970s offered many wonderful examples of the self-correcting nature of our democratic capitalism. Our society did some good things in the 1960s and 1970s, things that we can feel proud about as U.S. citizens, things that capitalism could never have accomplished. I mention these things because I want to discredit the notion that a bull market in government is axiomatically a bad thing. I hear that far too often around my office. A bull market in government is *not* axiomatically a bad thing. So, I want to review three changes that occurred in the 1960s where we-the-people made decisions that capitalism did not like but that made us a better people.

First, we-the-people declared that capitalism could not discriminate on the basis of race. We-the-people reaffirmed that we did indeed believe in the proposition that all men and women are created equal, and we-the-people, therefore, established within our rule of law a prohibition against discrimination on the basis of race. Capitalism would never have done that. We-the-people did it.

Second, we-the-people declared, "Thou shalt not discriminate on the basis of gender." Capitalism would never have come to that conclusion by itself. We-the-people did.

And third, we-the-people told capitalists, "Thou shalt not pollute and destroy our public property; that is, our environment. You must internalize in your profits the externalities of your behavior." We-the-people declared that some things are owned by all of us. These things constitute our collective property, which is, like private property, protected by the concept of property rights.

I am proud of these developments, and I think that most of us are proud as U.S. citizens that we took such measures in the 1960s and 1970s.

Three Power Shifts

The problem with the 1960s and 1970s was that after we-the-people made a number of decisions that capitalism would not have made on its own, the bull market in government drove capitalism into a bear market, which eventually led to Jimmy Carter appearing on national television in a cardigan sweater. It was time to shift the weights in our mixed economy from the public sector back toward the private sector. It was also time for some serious asset reallocation. Three power shifts occurred that helped create the market-based economy of the 1980s and 1990s—a shift in monetary policy, a shift in fiscal policy, and a shift in regulatory policy.

Monetary Policy. Jimmy Carter appointed Paul Volker chairman of the Federal Reserve in August 1979. On the same day, he effectively wrote his own pink slip and gave Mr. Volker a mandate to shift monetary policy from the political process to the markets. To make this shift, Mr. Volker had to do something that the Federal Reserve is supposed to be reluctant to do, and that is to throw our economy into recession. Recessions offend democratic sensibilities. Recessions do not inflict pain on an equitable basis. Recessions hurt the weakest among us, so the political process is naturally predisposed against tight monetary policy. But in 1978, the United States actually borrowed money to fund its current account deficit in nondollar currencies. These borrowed amounts became known as the Carter Bonds, and it was a sad day when the United States had to fund its current account deficit in a foreign currency. Because of developments such as this, the American people were willing to tolerate a recession to combat the nefarious inflationary problem they were facing. So, Paul Volker quit listening to the White House and started listening to what became known as the "bond market vigilantes," a term coined by Edward Yardeni, chief economist of Prudential Financial. In fact, one could argue that it was not so much the bond market vigilantes but the currency market vigilantes who turned the tide.

Fiscal Policy. The second power shift that laid the foundation for the market-based economy actually occurred in the 1990s under President Bill Clinton. We-the-people, for reasons that are still unclear to me, decided that we wanted to de-lever ourselves, to shift from budget deficits to budget surpluses and pay off our collective national debt. That is a very difficult thing for a democratic economy to do because a government that de-levers itself is a government that is reducing its own power. Typically, nobody likes to give up power. But giving up power is exactly what we-the-people did in the 1990s. There was, of course, an economic rationale to this delevering. Budget deficits crowd out private sector investment, and private sector investment, under the umbrella of capitalism, is inherently more productive than government sector investment. Therefore, reducing the budget deficit reduces the crowding out of private sector investment. Once the deficit was eliminated and the government started running surpluses, the government not only stopped crowding out private sector investment; it actually began crowding such investments in.

Regulatory Policy. The third power shift occurred in regulation, which is, in essence, a process by which we-the-people infringe on private sector property. I use the word "infringe" as a descriptor and not in a pejorative sense because regulation is not inherently bad. For example, assume you own a car, as do many people in the United States. You have a title for it in the glove compartment. It is your car, and your ownership is protected under property rights. But we-the-people do impose some regulations. We say, "Thou shalt not drive your car while you are drunk." That is a regulation, and most people would probably agree that it is a good regulation. We-the-people also say, "Thou shalt not drive your car faster than 65 miles per hour on the interstate." Many people feel less certain that this is a good regulation, as demonstrated by the fact that seven miles per hour over the speed limit seems to be the default standard.

My point is that regulation is not inherently bad. It can, however, go too far, as it had by the end of the 1970s. Therefore, a period of deregulation began. It began in the Carter administration with the deregulation of the airlines, which was followed by the deregulation of the financial system, the deregulation of the utilities, and finally, in 1996, the deregulation of the telephone companies. Deregulation thus restored private sector property rights.

Beer, Ballparks, and Disinflation. Put those three things together—tight money, fiscal discipline, and deregulation—and the result was the bull market in capitalism that, in turn, produced the variable that determined everything else—falling inflation. Capitalism is inherently disinflationary because capitalism is inherently about competition, which is a process of creative destruction. That is, under the framework of capitalism, no profit margin endures for long. Downward pressure on prices is naturally promoted.

As an example, consider one portion of the economy that was not deregulated during the 1980s and 1990s—the beer concessions at major league ballparks. No matter what ballpark a fan might visit, a beer costs $6.00. Why is this so? It is a regulated market. It is a market with a barrier to entry. It is a monopoly. It is not a capitalist market. Consider, therefore, what would happen if beer concessions were deregulated. Entrepreneurs would enter the market, and the sequence of events would go something like the following.

The first entrepreneur goes out and buys a pickup truck and a couple kegs of beer—called investment in GDP accounts—and begins offering beer at $5.50 per serving, not $6.00. This is called "disinflation," and assuming there is some price elasticity of demand, the consumption of beer rises. Thus, the economy experiences more investment, disinflation, and an increase in consumption. But other potential vendors say that a price of $5.50 per serving still provides an excess profit margin. So, another entrant appears and lowers the price of beer still more. Now, people become exuberant about the profit potential for selling beer at the ballpark. So, another entrepreneur enters the market and the price of a serving of beer drops to $4.00. At this point, venture capital discovers this wonderful profit-making opportunity, and entrants four, five, and six appear. Beer is now going for $2.25 per serving, and the first entrepreneur has gone public with an IPO. Exuberance is working. Inflation is going down, down, down.

The story finally ends with 17 guys selling beer at the ballpark for 25 cents a serving and a stadium full of drunks, which is exactly what happened to the telecom industry and the price of a long-distance phone call at the end of the 1990s. What was the cost of a long-distance phone call by the end of the 1990s? Not even a quarter.

Thus, shifting to a more capitalist model, tightening money, crowding in private sector investment, and deregulating industries led to falling inflation, which was the dominant theme of the 1980s and 1990s.

Five Strategies for Success in 1980. If an investment manager had understood the implications at the turn of the tide in 1980, he or she would have needed to do five things to be successful.

1. *Sell tangible assets into financial assets.* Falling inflation is inherently bearish for tangible assets versus financial assets. Disinflation is directly negative for pricing the product of tangible assets. Disinflation is directly positive for the valuation of stocks and bonds.
2. *Overweight stocks versus bonds.* The reason to sell financial assets into an overweighted portfolio in stocks is that disinflation and a bull market in capitalism have their most profound effect on the longest duration asset, which is equity.
3. *Overweight growth versus value.* A bull market in capitalism will take P/E multiples up because of falling inflation and the shifting of shares of GDP toward corporate profits. Investment managers will want a call option on the upside.
4. *Overweight government bonds versus corporate bonds.* This action may seem counterintuitive. Investment managers may think, "If we have a bull market in capitalism, shouldn't we be holding corporates?" But a bull market in capitalism, including the crowding in of private sector investment, means a crowding in of private sector default risk, so a bull market in capitalism is not bullish for corporate bonds.
5. *Overweight the U.S. dollar.* This move follows from the proposition that if the United States is going to have a party in celebration of capitalism, the rest of the world will want to attend the party and the cover charge for the party will be denominated in dollars.

If an investment manager did these five things in 1980, the resulting portfolio would look pretty good in 1990: light on tangible assets, long on financial assets, overweight on stocks, overweight on growth stocks, overweight on government bonds, and long on the dollar.

Capitalism's Cardigan Moment

The party celebrating capitalism was a great one, but all parties must come to an end, and so did this one. Whenever one sector of our mixed economy has been in power for too long, it suffers from hubris. Government suffered from hubris at the end of the 1970s; capitalism suffered from hubris at the end of the 1990s. The biggest source of hubris in capitalism at the end of the 1990s was that the marketplace convinced itself that the more capitalist an economy was, the gentler its business cycle would be. Therefore, by accepting the notion that capitalism would take the boom and bust out of our economy, the equity market reduced the equity risk premium to the point that it went negative. The reality, unfortunately, is that although capitalism can reduce inflation, it actually introduces more risk of boom and bust, as John Maynard Keynes explained in Chapter 12, "The State of Long-Term Expectation" (or "Animal Spirits," as the chapter is commonly called), of *The General Theory of Employment Interest and Money.*[1]

[1]John Maynard Keynes, *The General Theory of Employment Interest and Money* (Fort Washington, PA: Harvest Books, 1965).

Capitalism offers the opportunity to get rich, but it also requires the occasional duty of going broke. Socialism is inherently calmer in real time than capitalism. Therefore, if an economy moves toward a more capitalist system, its participants should expect a more agitated business cycle, not a calmer one. One of the redeeming characteristics of socialism is its calmness in real time. Just think in terms of the postal service or the department of motor vehicles. They offer no one the opportunity to get rich, but neither do they require anyone to go broke.

The problem with socialism, of course, is that it has revolutions every 50 years or so. Between revolutions it offers a fairly calm sort of existence, whereas capitalism presents us with a state of continuous revolution. The process is called "creative destruction," and it leads to periods of irrational exuberance and irrational doom. Capitalists involved in the equity market were confronted by capitalism's inherent instability when three bubbles burst at the end of the 1990s—the equity valuation bubble, the business investment bubble, and the corporate leverage bubble. Tobin's *q* predicted that an equity bubble would lead to a business investment bubble. Modigliani and Miller predicted that those two bubbles would lead to a corporate debt bubble. All three occurred as predicted, and all three burst just as the economy reached the end of a welcomed disinflation.

Thus, we saw a unique inflection point because the bubbles burst at a 2 percent inflation rate, which means that the economy had a fundamental need to reflate. Otherwise, the economy would have been in danger of a Minsky-style debt deflation, which occurs when the entire corporate sector decides to rehabilitate its balance sheet.[2] For individual companies, such a decision represents rational behavior. Collectively, however, it embodies the paradox of thrift: Not all companies can rehabilitate their balance sheets at the same time. Nevertheless, that is exactly what the corporate sector tried to do, and it introduced the distinct risk of a deflationary spiral, which was the point at which a new bull market in government was born.

Three Power Shifts in Reverse. That we are, in fact, living in a bull market in government can be demonstrated by examining the reverse of the three power shifts that I discussed earlier—shifts in monetary policy, fiscal policy, and regulation.

- *Monetary policy*. Monetary policy is under the guidance of Federal Reserve Board Chairman Alan Greenspan. During the past three years, Mr. Greenspan has not been listening to the bond market vigilantes, nor has he been listening to the currency market vigilantes. Monetary policy in the United States is geared quite appropriately toward saving capitalism from its deflationary self by reflating. The power of the printing press, which we-the-people own, has now been turned to generating higher inflation.
- *Fiscal policy*. Fortunately for the United States, we-the-people have forgotten that nonsense about de-levering ourselves, and we have shifted from a budget surplus to a huge budget deficit. The United States is re-levering itself, which is precisely what is needed when the private sector is trying to de-lever itself. So, the Federal Reserve is printing $20 bills and the federal government is borrowing $20 bills.
- *Regulation*. The United States is re-regulating along a number of fronts, but the one that seems most significant is embodied in the Sarbanes–Oxley Act of 2002, which regulates corporate governance. Sarbanes–Oxley is the anti-drunk-driving bill for CEOs. It states, in effect, "Thou shalt not drive the car of American capitalism while drunk with hubris and greed. If you do, your pinstripes will no longer be vertically aligned but will be horizontally aligned."

Capitalism's hubris exposed the United States to deflation risk, and it offended our democratic sensibilities. We are now in a corrective process.

Five Strategies in an Era of Inflation

Assuming that I am right and that the United States is at an inflection point from which capitalism is in retreat and the power of we-the-people is in ascendancy, it is fair to conclude, on a secular horizon, that inflation will rise. I have no idea what the U.S. Consumer Price Index will be next week, next month, or next year. But if we have indeed reached the antithesis of 1981, then inflation is going to go up, and that development holds many implications for investment portfolios. Investment managers will need to reverse the five strategies needed for success in 1980, thus realigning their portfolios to a mix of public and private sector investments that better matches the macroeconomic environment.

1. *Overweight tangible assets versus financial assets*. If we are indeed entering a we-the-people bull market and secularly rising inflation, a successful portfolio will need more tangible assets.
2. *Balance stocks and bonds*. Unfortunately, both stocks and bonds are going to offer lousy returns in the years ahead because rising inflation is both a headwind to P/E multiples and a corrosive for total returns on bonds. Stocks and bonds had their glorious two-decade run, but now they face a headwind. If I were forced to choose, I would overweight bonds versus stocks, partly because

[2]Hyman Minsky, *Stabilizing an Unstable Economy* (New Haven, CT: Yale University Press, 1986).

I consider stocks to be a call option on capitalism. If capitalism is checked into the Betty Ford Center for balance sheet rehabilitation, the call option is not worth as much.

3. *Overweight value versus growth*. The coming environment is not one in which growth stocks will perform well. They have outperformed during the past year because the rally of the past year has been about the nation re-embracing the American enterprise as a going concern. But we must now think in terms of normalized relative valuations and performance, which means a bias toward value.
4. *Overweight private sector obligations*. A bull market in government is actually a bull market in credit quality. Current valuations are rich in the corporate bond market but, secularly speaking, investors should shift from government debt to private debt.
5. *Overweight nondollar assets versus the dollar*. In the United States, rising inflation and a more government-controlled economy will act as secular anvils on the dollar's value. What is more, the sheer size of the U.S. current account deficit—an inevitable consequence of "successful" reflation—implies a surplus of dollars globally relative to private global demand.

Conclusion

Based on the lessons of history, success in portfolio management depends on adjusting appropriately to the prospective weights in our mixed economy, not to the weights as they used to exist. Investment managers cannot afford to extrapolate from the returns of the prior regime to project returns into a future regime. The returns of the 1980s and 1990s arose from a bull market in capitalism and falling inflation, and those conditions do not appear on the secular horizon. If investment managers take seriously their fiduciary mandate to anticipate the future and not simply extrapolate from the past, they cannot use the returns of the 1980s and 1990s as the foundation for a prudent, forward-looking efficient frontier.

Question and Answer Session

Paul McCulley

Question: From the standpoint of generations, we-the-people is not monolithic. What is the point of inflection for large, long-term, abstract risks, such as Fannie Mae risks and Social Security liabilities, which we-the-people do not want to acknowledge, manage, or pay for?

McCulley: We-the-people is indeed not monolithic. It is made up of old people and young people. We have made commitments to the old people in our society, and that is going to be a daunting burden for us to carry. Mr. Greenspan spoke of it recently. We all talk about it. Unfortunately, we-the-people have promised more than we can deliver for our aging population, and I believe that I can forecast with a high degree of certainty that the real value of the promises we have made to our retired population is going to erode.

Such erosion is likely to occur in one of two ways. We can cut the nominal benefits, or we can run higher-than-expected inflation. One or the other must happen because our system of retirement and, more important, our system of medical care have not adjusted to two realities—demographics and technology. We are having fewer children, which means that the ratio of young to old people is moving in the wrong direction. Furthermore, technology is allowing us to live longer. Ultimately, we will have to address those issues because the younger generation has been given a burden it cannot bear. We are facing the unfortunate paradox that our long and healthy lives are going to make others' lives more difficult in the future. The easiest solution is for everyone to start smoking again. But God bless America; I want to live a long time.

Question: Is the capitalist party over, or is it simply moving from the small parlor of North America to the much larger and more raucous rec room of Asia?

McCulley: I think the party is moving, although when I look at Asia, democratic capitalism is not exactly what comes to mind. But the economies there are pretty thoroughly market based. In the years ahead, outsourcing will remain as a dominant political issue because China will cause a positive supply-side shock in the global economy as it continues making the transition from a command economy to a market economy. The global supply curve of labor will shift, which is a marvelous thing for consumers because we will ultimately have a more extensive menu from which to shop. Thus, as capitalism in Asia grows more vibrant, protectionist pressures in the United States will become more intense. That is neither good nor bad; it is just a natural outcome of the fact that we have free trade in global goods and services, but we do not have free trade in global labor.

Rethinking Boundaries and Achieving Greater Flexibility in Implementing the Policy Portfolio

Richard M. Ennis, CFA
Principal
Ennis, Knupp & Associates
Chicago

A growing number of investors has become interested in introducing greater flexibility into their policy portfolios. This flexibility can be accomplished in several ways, such as giving managers broader mandates or eliminating the long-only constraint. A more comprehensive approach would be to separate how investors get the return of the policy portfolio (beta) from how they seek to exploit security mispricing (alpha). For that approach to work, more large funds need to develop stronger capabilities, more institutional-quality managers need to offer alpha-only strategies, and "master managers" need to enter the market. The master manager would be a hybrid of indexer, overlay manager, transition manager, master custodian, and consultant with the role of facilitating advanced forms of institutional portfolio management.

A policy portfolio splices together component benchmarks in the same proportions as the investor's target allocation to various asset classes. Thus, it forms a total-fund benchmark that approximates passive implementation of the overall investment policy.

The policy portfolio is an important construct and likely to endure as a best practice in institutional fund management because it preserves an important distinction in the function of portfolio management. The first goal of portfolio management is to infuse the portfolio with the proper sense of the investor's liabilities, objectives, and risk tolerance. These characteristics are fundamental and enduring and warrant a certain allegiance. At the same time, and secondarily, portfolio management affords investors an opportunity to exploit security mispricing, which tends to be elusive.

By monitoring portfolio composition relative to the policy portfolio, the investor ensures that implementation does not stray from his or her circumstances. Risk budgeting, in which active risk is controlled in aggregate and parsed among sources, is the most recent refinement to the policy portfolio's *control function*. And by comparing the actual return with that of the policy portfolio after the fact, the investor can isolate the effect of active management to evaluate its efficacy. This is the policy portfolio's *performance measurement function*.

Why the Interest in Greater Flexibility Now?

Peter Bernstein touched on a theme that is stirring considerable interest and controversy in the profession—the idea of achieving greater flexibility in implementing the policy portfolio.[1] But what accounts for the current interest in achieving greater investment flexibility?

Acknowledging the Futility of Closet Indexing. The standard implementation model for large pension funds during the 1980s and 1990s was to employ a large number of managers—often upwards of 20—within narrow asset class specialties. Most managers diversify within their area of specialization, be it large-cap growth stocks in the United

[1] See Peter L. Bernstein, "Points of Inflection: Investment Management Tomorrow," *Financial Analysts Journal* (July/August 2003):18–23.

States, emerging market stocks, or a segment of the bond market. In the spirit of risk control, clients, with the help of their consultants, fashioned complex mosaics of manager style, superimposing a largely fixed template of style and factor diversification on the managers' security-level diversification. The result was a form of implementation high in rigidity and cost—and, in the aggregate, low in active risk. It was aptly dubbed "closet indexing." I cannot help but believe that disaffection with closet indexing has contributed to the interest in greater flexibility.

Evolution of Instruments and Markets. The introduction of new trading instruments and the evolution of markets have expanded opportunities to create portfolio exposures and lower transaction costs. Ever greater investment flexibility is a by-product of this innovation.

Globalization. Globalization has contributed to greater integration of investment markets. Stock market sector factors are now at least as important as country of domicile in explaining stock returns. The distinction between "domestic" and "foreign" blurred as such companies as Daimler and Chrysler merged and competition generally took on a truly international character. Markets that were "emerging" have been reclassified as "developed" and vice versa. European countries now share a common currency. Market segmentation everywhere is vanishing in the name of economic efficiency. And globalization demands a less parochial, more flexible approach to investing.

The Bubble. As the Internet telecommunications bubble formed, investors witnessed IPOs blowing through small- and mid-cap space to become large-cap growth companies virtually overnight. Large-cap growth indexes, which traditionally contained a relative few percentage points of technology stocks, came to be dominated by tech. Traditional stock managers were challenged to change their spots and adjust their styles to the new economy or risk being rendered obsolete. At the same time, spectacular distortions in valuation created opportunity for those less inhibited by the strictures of style: Managers willing and able to shift from growth to value in 2000 profited handsomely. Hedge funds, as a class, played the bubble just about right, effectively eliminating significant net-long equity exposures near the top. And so, in all likelihood, and for better or worse, the bubble and its aftermath have contributed to a newfound spirit of opportunism.

A Perceived Disconnect between Risk and Expected Return. Bubble pricing brought forth an outpouring of critical thinking about the equity risk premium. Thoughtful observers questioned how stocks, yielding barely more than 1 percent and remaining at exceptional multiples by historical standards even after the bubble burst, could produce a satisfactory—or even positive—real return in the years ahead. Some approached the matter with scholarly rigor whereas others were more matter of fact. Warren Buffett, for example, observed late in 1999, with bonds yielding 6.7 percent, that the stock market looked like a fine place to earn about 6 percent a year for the foreseeable future.

In its most vigorous expression, concern over the equity risk premium is nothing less than a perceived breakdown in the pricing of assets, a view that stocks are not priced to provide an appropriate return for the risk they entail. In a world such as this, were it to exist, a large and fixed allocation to equities would have no place in portfolio management.

The Rise of the Hedge Fund. Hedge funds epitomize investment flexibility, and their proliferation in the past 10 years has been spectacular. The growing acceptance of hedge funds, although in and of itself not an impetus for more flexibility, has become a strong source of collateral support. Thus, one might best describe the popularization of hedge funds as a manifestation of the enthusiasm for more flexible approaches.

Caveats. Some of these reasons are good ones for seeking greater flexibility. Scrapping the use of active managers for diversification—closet indexing—is one of them. Recognizing that skill is not necessarily narrow in scope and that markets are increasingly integrated also strikes me as worthy justification for rethinking the investment approach. And if the introduction of instruments and the evolution of markets increase flexibility, investors will certainly avail themselves of it.

Other arguments for greater flexibility warrant careful examination. As a secular outlook, believing that stocks will do no better than bonds is to suggest that the market is cockeyed relative to long-term history. The view that bonds will do better than stocks is a shorter-term market outlook. Skillful execution can be profitable, to be sure, but significant risks exist as well. In 2003, the S&P 500 Index produced a return of 26 percent and the Lehman Brothers Aggregate Bond Index returned 4 percent, for an equity-over-bond premium of 22 percent. This outcome is inconsistent with the no-equity-risk-premium view prevailing in late 2002. Investors who shifted heavily from stocks to bonds based on such an outlook suffered dearly. Betting against the equity risk premium is a strategy narrow in breadth, making both skill and risk control of paramount importance.

I hasten to add that I am not making a market forecast of any kind. Rather, I am simply reminding investors of a fundamental tenet: For purposes of investment policy planning, expected return and market risk go hand in hand.

A truly specious justification for promoting greater investment flexibility is the notion that market returns in this low-inflation, low-interest-rate environment no longer meet the "requirements" of investors and that the only way to make up the difference is by garnering alpha. Let me be clear: Positive alphas go to those who can earn them and to those who are lucky. They are not distributed based on investors' appetite for them, which brings me to the question of the hour: Can investors achieve greater flexibility in implementing investment policy without undermining the very function of investment policy?

Achieving Greater Flexibility Wisely

Institutional investors vary in asset size, resources, and sophistication. Accordingly, techniques that make sense for a $10 billion educational endowment or a $50 billion pension fund are simply not available to a $100 million fund. I believe, however, that opportunities abound for becoming more flexible in implementing the policy portfolio for all types of investors. I will begin by discussing the simpler, more universal ways to accomplish this task and progress to the more advanced.

Fewer Managers, Broader Mandates. To the extent that investment skill exists, I do not believe it is purely local, so to speak, existing only—or even primarily—in connection with the appraisal of a relatively short list of homogeneous securities. Nor do I believe markets are so inefficient that institutional investors can expect to profit from hiring dozens of conventional long-only, stylized specialists. Indeed, I maintain that funds have employed large numbers of such managers because they lack confidence in their ability to select those who will prove skillful.

I do believe investment opportunity is sometimes here, and sometimes there, and that skillful managers should be free to find it where it lies. And I believe some skillful managers can and do benefit from the perspective and latitude that a broad purview affords them.

The type of rigid specialization to which I object is more characteristic of domestic equity portfolio management than it is of international equity or fixed-income portfolio management. Those areas have evolved more along the *whole-portfolio* lines that I favor for conventional investment management. Core-plus managers work in and among all bond market sectors, and non-U.S. equity managers invest literally all over the map. Thus, a prime area of opportunity for achieving greater flexibility in implementation is the domestic equity portfolio.

And do not overlook the opportunity to break down the arbitrary boundary that exists between "domestic" and "non-U.S." markets. Evidence of global integration indicates that this rigid distinction is just not right. Investors can and should be giving greater credence to global equity portfolio management.

Employing fewer managers with broader mandates is a relatively easy, reasonably conservative way to render implementation more flexible while reducing, rather than increasing, complexity. In this sense, it is a good place for most funds to start.

Eliminating the Long-Only Constraint. Let me be clear that all this talk of greater flexibility has to do with exploiting security mispricing. Investors can get any form of market exposure they want reliably and cheaply with passive portfolios and derivatives. As for mispricing, overpriced securities should be as interesting to investors as underpriced securities, which raises the specter of short selling.

Portfolio-improvement opportunities increase significantly when the long-only constraint is removed. Relaxing the long-only constraint contributes to portfolio efficiency in two ways:

- It enables the manager to underweight an overvalued security by a margin larger than its weight in the benchmark, and
- For a given amount of capital, it permits larger overweights in underpriced assets.

Figure 1 illustrates the gain in active return for various levels of active risk when the constraint is relaxed. Under the assumptions used in the figure, with active risk of 5 percent, the increase in alpha is more than 200 bps.

Thus, skillful long–short managers have an edge over long-only managers, all else being equal, which is an argument in favor of including managers unencumbered by the long-only constraint.

Note, however, that short selling is associated with limitations, costs, and frictions that can prove severely restrictive for some strategies, revealing once again the limits of arbitrage. With time, the evolution of markets may lessen them. In this respect, the U.S. SEC's proposal to do away with the up-tick rule is a promising sign; and some electronic communication networks, by the way, are already exempt from that rule.

Figure 1. Active-Return Gain from Relaxing Long-Only Constraint

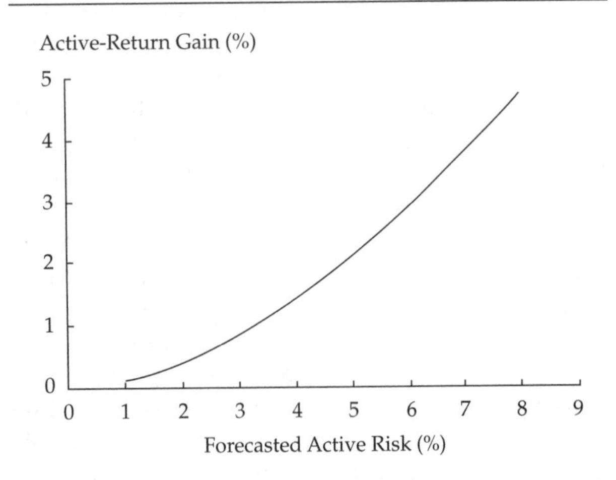

Note: Based on a portfolio of 50 stocks and an information ratio equal to 1.5.

Source: Based on data from Richard C. Grinold and Ronald N. Kahn, "The Efficiency Gains of Long–Short Investing," *Financial Analysts Journal* (November/December 2000):40–53.

Separating Strategic Allocation and Diversification from Value-Added Investing. Traditionally, alpha has been lost in the shuffle with beta. This outcome is true even for hedge funds, where research indicates that 44 percent of diversified hedge fund exposures is directional and that up to 80 percent of the return variation is market related.[2] In the industry's jargon, beta is being sold as alpha, even among hedge funds.

Increasingly, investors hear that the ultimate in refining portfolio management is *separating how they get the return of the policy portfolio from how they seek to exploit security mispricing*. One important goal here is to pay passive-management fees for the return of the policy portfolio and active-management fees solely for alpha generation. Another goal is to be in a position to select managers with the highest prospective information ratios without regard to asset class considerations. In principle, here lies the ultimate flexibility in implementing the policy portfolio.

Although investors hear a great deal about so-called portable-alpha schemes nowadays, they are uncommon in practice and, at best, piecemeal in operation. Implementation remains a big problem. Scraping alphas clean of their associated betas is easier said than done. The technology and instruments to do so remain esoteric for now, and very few funds have the knowledge and resources to manage their portfolios this way. Furthermore, some of the relevant instruments are not sufficiently liquid.

Convention is another hurdle. Investors are accustomed to thinking in terms of asset classes, in implementation as well as policy design. And the prospect of a derivatives-laden portfolio only serves to raise the hurdle of acceptance for many fiduciaries.

In the interest of accelerating the advancement of the state of the art in the investment industry, I take this opportunity to introduce and advocate a new concept in money management—the "master manager."

To appreciate what follows, readers will have to let their imagination run a bit. The master manager is a hybrid of indexer, overlay manager, transition manager, master custodian, and consultant. The master manager does not necessarily replace these functions entirely, but it does combine elements of all of them. The master manager is also a not-so-distant cousin of the "new-paradigm" manager Charles Ellis advocated more than a decade ago. *The role of the master manager is to facilitate advanced forms of institutional portfolio management.* This new breed of manager would perform these functions for a pension or endowment fund:

1. *The master manager implements the marketable securities component of the client's policy portfolio using index funds, exchanged-traded funds, and derivatives as cheaply as possible.* In this respect, the master manager is a macro-passive manager, using all the media available.
2. *The master manager makes cash or securities available from time to time to fund active managers of the client's choosing.* It does this, for example, by using futures to gain exposure to certain market sectors and withdrawing the free cash to fund a new manager. Or it may conduct a transition from a passive portfolio to an active one. For very large funds—those with separate-account index funds—the master manager may be able to lessen the cost of borrowing shares for short sales by lending them directly from passive portfolios.
3. *The master manager monitors risk and compliance of active portfolios, which is not an uncommon function of master trustees and overlay managers.*
4. *The master manager neutralizes any unintended factor exposures, including leverage.* The client may appoint active managers who are strictly market neutral, leaving as the only factor exposures those of the policy portfolio. In the more likely event that some managers bring factor exposures, such as a stock market beta, a value bias, or unwanted leverage, the master manager is in a position to adapt its portfolio to them in the spirit of completeness investing. This is a feature Barton Waring has dubbed "portable beta."[3]

[2]See Richard M. Ennis and Michael D. Sebastian, "A Critical Look at the Case for Hedge Funds," *Journal of Portfolio Management* (Summer 2003):103–112.

[3]See Barton Waring's presentation in this proceedings.

5. *The master manager rebalances in accordance with the client's direction to preserve the character of the policy portfolio and balance the active-risk budget.* In this capacity, the master manager is in a good position to help the client evaluate the trade-off between tracking error and transaction costs.

The master manager requires exceptional capabilities of three types—analytical, trading, and operational. It does not, however, use skill in the sense of accurately forecasting security mispricing. Rather, it offers a fully integrated platform for the client to pursue alpha independent of the business of getting the policy portfolio return.

Two challenges face the investor seeking alpha independently of the policy portfolio return. One is cost. Alpha-only strategies are priced richer than conventional investment management, with higher base fees plus profit participation. It also comes with the cost of attempting to separate alpha from beta and maintaining the desired risk exposures, and employing a master manager may involve additional fees. It is important to note that very large funds can internalize the master management function as a way of controlling cost.

A second challenge is making an accurate assessment of the factor exposures of the active managers. With traditional long-only portfolios, this assessment may not be a problem. It can be a problem, however, for managers not offering complete transparency of their holdings.

Summary

The policy portfolio serves a critical function in fund management; it is here to stay. Greater flexibility in implementing the policy portfolio is of interest to those—and only to those—who can select skillful active managers. Broadening mandates and relaxing the long-only constraint are two sensible ways to introduce greater flexibility, although short sellers face constraints of their own. The ultimate flexibility is attained when investors separate altogether the way they get the return of the policy portfolio from the way they seek active returns. Today, doing so is easier said than done.

For the approach to take hold, I believe three developments need to occur:

- More large funds need to develop internally the capabilities required to separate alpha from beta;
- More managers of institutional caliber need to offer alpha-only strategies; and
- At least a few master managers need to enter the scene.

Question and Answer Session

Richard M. Ennis, CFA

Question: Why has it taken so long in the investment management industry to move in the direction of flexible mandates?

Ennis: I think funds have been understandably cautious. They became persuaded by the research of the 1970s and early 1980s about the efficiency of markets and the difficulties of trying to beat the market. I believe the rigidity that has evolved is in part a function of that way of thinking (i.e., it is a form of risk control). It is also a part of the function of the way the investment management community transacts with the buying community. It creates a product that fits niches, which in itself contributes to rigidity.

Question: How can we practically execute a portable alpha and beta approach given institutional reluctance to use leverage and derivatives and the practice of defining hedge funds as a separate asset class in the policy portfolio?

Ennis: I'm troubled by putting hedge funds in the policy allocation of portfolios. I do not know how to do that. It is not an asset class. It doesn't have characteristics that we can attribute. It is a management effect, so we don't try to do that. The solution that I've come up with to overcome the difficulties of separating the two is to get help from some of the large financial institutions that I believe are in a better position to do this separation process—work with master trustees and large indexers and overlay managers and transition managers and do their own completeness analytical work. I see a fund industry that is getting the concept but simply lacks the means to execute it. Will this work? I don't know, but if this approach doesn't help us, I suspect nothing will. It is a complex business right now.

Question: With fewer managers, aren't you narrowing your breadth and thus potentially lowering your expected information ratio?

Ennis: I would suggest seeking breadth in the particular strategies that are used. I'm all for taking advantage of breadth, but I think it can occur *within* the various strategies that are used. If you are able to select as few as 10 active strategies that are uncorrelated, they're going to substantially eliminate your active-management risk. I think we haven't fully examined that notion. I don't think we need "breadth" in the sense of a large number of investment managers to get investment breadth in the Grinold and Kahn sense.

Question: Are any firms currently ramping up for this master manager concept? And what's your anticipation about the fees the new master managers will charge for these services on top of the fees for the management process itself?

Ennis: We're having discussions currently with three large integrated organizations, integrated with indexing and custody, and they have exhibited a high degree of interest in filling this role. This is not exactly a revolutionary notion because most of these institutions have these capabilities. They simply haven't been asked to package them in this fashion. So, the three organizations we've begun talking to have exhibited not only enthusiasm but also confidence in their ability to fill this function.

In terms of pricing, we haven't gotten that far yet. My theory is the pricing would be something equivalent to a passive-management fee for the total portfolio plus some kind of premium.

Question: Isn't a master portfolio just a variant of an asset allocation policy?

Ennis: It certainly incorporates all of the functions of asset allocation and rebalancing and risk control, but it does so more in an operational sense, not in a design sense. This is an operational concept.

Question: Who in the marketplace now would you describe as a master manager?

Ennis: The candidates would include large integrated indexers and custodians, such as Barclays Global Investors, Mellon Capital Management Corporation, Northern Trust Corporation, State Street Corporation, and others of that ilk that have significant passive portfolio capabilities and have developed other types of capabilities as ancillary services. I also think that plenty of opportunity exists for other types of firms. For example, I think that a number of firms specializing in active asset allocation and overlay management could step into this role.

Question: Which hedge fund styles offer alpha versus some odd combination of betas?

Ennis: I don't think you can generalize about that. I think individual funds offer alphas, positive or negative. I guess if there's one premise that underlies my work, it is that manager selection should be made unconditional with respect to categories.

Question: How do you measure skill with hedge funds?

Ennis: At Ennis, Knupp & Associates, we look at hedge fund returns using Bill Sharpe's returns-based style analysis. We make some adjustments in the methodology to allow for the use of short positions, and we relax the budget constraints so everything doesn't have to add up to 100 percent. Then, we look at a return series. We look across a whole host of factors where there are significant betas. We then identify those betas, the factor exposures, that appear to be statistically significant. At that point, we rerun our analysis eliminating the other, not significant factors. We then look at the alpha associated with that analysis. That is the way we both characterize the factor exposures and separate the alpha from the beta.

Question: How is the after-tax efficiency of a long-only strategy adversely affected by introducing short selling with its higher turnover and costs (market impact and borrowing costs) and differential tax treatment?

Ennis: I have been spending some time mulling that issue over myself because there is the potential for significant tax issues. It boils down to realizing that the harder we have to work to get that precious alpha, the more we are going to have to acknowledge that taxes are a secondary consideration.

Question: How much additional risk will a fund take on by eliminating the long-only constraint?

Ennis: To start, we put more emphasis on transparency than some others might. We are ultimately looking for managers with sophisticated risk controls that we can observe. With a long–short market-neutral strategy, we want to see how the balancing of assets occurs, how the balancing of betas occurs, and perhaps even diversification by industry and sector. Leverage is, of course, also a concern. But I do not believe that long–short market-neutral strategies necessarily have a propensity to blow up more than long-only strategies. More important, through diversification among the strategies, risk budgeting can be accomplished just as well as with long-only strategies.

Question: How do you identify skillful managers beforehand, and how do you judge their success after the fact?

Ennis: After the fact I would do it the way I described previously, by identifying the beta exposures that are not transitory and making adjustments for them to determine the net alpha. Beforehand identification, however, is quite difficult.

What you do not do is start by looking in categories. You also do not start by looking at managers' track records. I am of the old school that says past performance stinks as a means of forecasting future performance. At Ennis, Knupp & Associates, we have identified a system. To summarize it, we have about eight factors for evaluating investment managers. Number one, and the one that is weighted most heavily, is skill. We look for someone with an edge who is doing something that is plausible as a basis for adding value. Other factors include such things as portfolio trading efficiency, usage of soft dollars, or recent ownership changes in the organization. As one of the eight factors, we include past performance at a weighting of 15 percent. Ultimately, to the extent that you can shift the focus away from past performance, you are off to a good start.

If you are interested in more detail, we have a thorough description of our system on our company's website.[1]

Question: Verizon Communications launched an approach to management in the 1990s in which it employed an array of managers with broad flexibility to a policy portfolio. How does that approach compare with your master management approach?

Ennis: That is interesting. I believe that approach originated with GTE Corporation (Verizon Communications was formed by the merger of GTE and Bell Atlantic). If I remember correctly, they were hiring managers who could invest all over the map in stocks and bonds, both domestically and internationally. I have not looked at it in quite a while. The last time I checked on it was about a year ago, and at least at that time the approach had produced favorable results.

That strategy is not so much an example of what I refer to as this master manager concept. Rather, it is more an example of the ultimate whole-portfolio manager that I talked about as well. It is an example of freeing the manager of shackles so he or she can seek out value wherever it is likely to be found. I think it is a terrific idea, and I would encourage more groups to look at strategies with wider boundaries.

[1]See www.ennisknupp.com/.

Distinguishing True Alpha from Beta

Laurence B. Siegel
Director, Investment Policy Research
The Ford Foundation
New York City

Portfolios can be thought of as being composed of a beta component, which is broad asset class exposure, and an alpha component, which is excess return achieved through active management. If investors are hiring active managers, presumably because they believe these managers have real skill or the ability to deliver alpha, then they ought to be sure that they are paying for true alpha and not beta. These principles are not only applicable to traditional institutional portfolios, such as defined-benefit plans and endowments, but are also relevant for nontraditional portfolios, such as hedge funds.

Will Rogers was, among other things, a legendary investor of his personal assets and the first absolute-return investor. His advice to other investors was to: "Buy some good stock and hold it til it goes up, then sell it. If it don't go up, don't buy it."

He was kidding as usual, but a couple of generations ago many long-only managers talked like that, and they were not kidding. They said: "We are absolute-return investors. We just buy stocks that go up. We do not care what the market is doing." Now, a new crop of people who were not born back then are saying the same thing about hedge funds.

In 1964, long-only investors who imagined themselves to be absolute-return investors were set straight by Bill Sharpe when he showed statistically how to separate the policy risk (which he called "beta") from the active risk (which he called "alpha"). His approach caught on fairly quickly, and 10 or 20 years later, most long-only managers had their tail between their legs and were quoting the alphas they had produced, not their absolute returns that included the market or index component. If their alphas were negative, then the consultants punished them by advising clients to invest with another manager. That kind of benchmarking has added a discipline to the market that it desperately needed. Without benchmarking, investors would wind up paying alpha-type fees, active fees, for the index part of the return. Given some advances in measurement, this practice can also be applied to alternative investments, where the beta exposures are not quite as obvious.

Skill in the investment management industry is a rare commodity. The average market participant may be an intelligent individual, but by definition, this average participant cannot beat the average. And because the average return of all market participants can be achieved at very low cost by buying an index fund, an active manager has to be better than average to add alpha. In other words, many investors are better served by investing in a passively managed index fund than by investing with an active manager and taking the risk that the manager has less skill than average and will thus have a negative alpha.

In this presentation, I will try to make sense of this principle and will focus on the distinction between active or alpha risk, which is the risk taken to beat a benchmark, and policy or beta risk, which is the risk taken by merely investing in the benchmark. I will first discuss some general principles that I call the "dimensions of active management" in reference to an article I coauthored with Barton Waring.[1] Then, I will discuss applying those concepts to alternative investments, such as hedge funds, because that subject is of intense interest to so many people right now. Finally, I will talk about policy implications for pension funds and other investors.

[1] M. Barton Waring and Laurence B. Siegel, "The Dimensions of Active Management," *Journal of Portfolio Management* (Spring 2003):35–51.

The Dimensions of Active Management

Active management has three dimensions:

- pure active return, which is the value added by the manager (or what should be properly called alpha),
- pure active risk, which is the volatility of the pure active return, and
- costs.

A manager does not have absolute control over all three of these dimensions. A manager does not control return; it comes or it does not, according to how the markets perform. An element of control is associated with active risk. Costs, however, are the dimension that a manager directly controls. If a manager wants to add to his or her return, cutting active management fees would be one way of doing so, but cutting costs will not help if the costs pay for actual alpha being delivered on a consistent basis. That cost is worth the money.

A Portfolio of Betas and a Portfolio of Alphas. When investment performance is considered in the three dimensions of return, risk, and cost, a number of puzzle pieces emerge. The first one is taught in business school, but people tend not to apply it: Policy risk and active risk are separable and should be separated. They should really be thought of as two distinct portfolios. One is a portfolio of betas and consumes 100 percent of the capital. It is a portfolio of exposures to various market risk factors, which can conveniently be thought of as index funds, although the investor might be able to invest in futures or exchange-traded funds (ETFs) or something other than traditional index funds. For simplicity, think of it as 100 percent of capital being consumed through bets on various index funds.

The other portfolio is a self-financing portfolio of alphas. It consumes no capital. Theoretically, an investor should be able to earn alpha anywhere in any asset class through a long–short strategy that does not involve using the investor's own capital. The portfolio of alphas should be designed based on where the investor can best earn alpha or best earn a high information ratio (IR), which is the alpha per unit of active risk taken. That mix of assets should have nothing to do with the mix of assets in the portfolio of betas, which should be structured based on the investor's liabilities.

Investing in this way may not always be practical. But the separation of alpha and beta—what is sometimes called portable alpha—is at least a sound conceptual way of thinking about one's portfolio.

Pure Alpha and Naive Alpha. When measuring alpha, differentiating between pure alpha and naive alpha is important. A lot of investment managers subtract the return of the benchmark from the return of their portfolio and then call the remainder alpha. They have not made an adjustment for beta, so this approach does not demonstrate real alpha. Real alpha must be estimated from a regression. Bill Sharpe's market model regression is similar to the capital asset pricing model (CAPM), so most people call it the CAPM regression. That is the first step.

The next step is to see if any other systematic factors in the returns properly belong to the beta category rather than the alpha category. The factors that generally turn out to be meaningful are the two common style factors known as "value minus growth" and "small cap minus large cap." If a manager adjusts for all these common factors and for the beta of the overall portfolio relative to the market, then he or she has isolated the true alpha, the pure alpha, for which active managers should be paid. All the other exposures belong in the portfolio of betas and should reap index fund–like fees.

Style Boxes. Style boxes do not do a good job of categorizing managers. A growth manager who concentrates in the most rapidly growing companies, or a value manager who is more price conscious than most, will not tend to be close to the center of his or her growth or value style box. Thinking of such managers as fitting into these boxes misrepresents managers and affects the style allocations in a negative way. A much better way of thinking about managers is to use a style map that creates a continuum from growth to value, from large to small cap, from zero beta to some beta higher than 1. In this space, a manager represents a point. In other words, the manager can be anywhere on the continuum in any of these dimensions.

Manager Structure Optimization. Having identified the location of each candidate manager on the style map through style analysis, one can then build a portfolio of managers through optimization. As Barton Waring and I discussed in "The Dimensions of Active Management," building a portfolio of managers is like building a portfolio of anything: It is an optimization problem, although it is a little trickier than conventional optimization because it has two stages. One stage is for the portfolio of betas, and the other is for the portfolio of alphas. We refer to the optimization for the portfolio of alphas as "manager structure optimization." To do that optimization, investors require estimates of expected alphas and expected active risk (or tracking error) for managers in exactly the same way they need estimates of the risk and return of the asset classes for the portfolio of betas.

Estimating Expected Alphas for Managers. Estimating expected alphas for managers can be a struggle; many people do not know how to do it. But these expected alphas are already in their portfolios. Through reverse optimization, one can easily calculate the expected alpha implied by the weight the manager has in the portfolio. So, if people do not think they can estimate expected alphas for managers, surprise—they are already doing it.

Constructing the alpha estimates needed to build an efficient portfolio of managers is, without a doubt, difficult. There is no formula or recipe for estimating expected alphas. Each investor has to come up with a way to estimate those numbers, and a particular investor's approach may not necessarily rely on quantitative methods. If an investor is going to justify holding active managers rather than index funds, however, then the investor should be able to quantify the expectation that the manager will earn alpha. If the investor can do that, then a manager structure optimizer can be used to build an optimal portfolio of managers.

Barclays Global Investors has written software to perform manager structure optimization. I have experimented with the software a little bit, and it gives surprisingly neat results. Although it sounds like a mostly theoretical experiment, it is not. The software produces portfolios of managers that are plausible and not subject to the common critique that optimizers are mostly garbage-in, garbage-out machines; the output is actually useful.

Two Conditions for Selecting Active Managers. As I have said, active management should not be expected to win just because it is active; it is a zero-sum game, with winners counterbalanced by losers (and that is before deducting costs). As a result, an investor has to satisfy two conditions for it to be rational to play the active management game. The first is that the investor has to believe that there are some active managers with real skill who add value other than just by chance. The second condition, which is the tougher one, is that the investor has to believe that he or she can pick these exceptional managers from a large population of managers who are mostly not exceptional.

Those who meet the second condition should indeed hire active managers and might like to know what a portfolio looks like that reflects the principles I have been describing. If an investor is constrained to be long-only, then the portfolio must be constructed from managers on the bottom curve in **Figure 1**. Managers on this curve include index funds, enhanced index funds, and traditional active funds (both concentrated and diversified).

Figure 1. Impact of the Long-Only Constraint

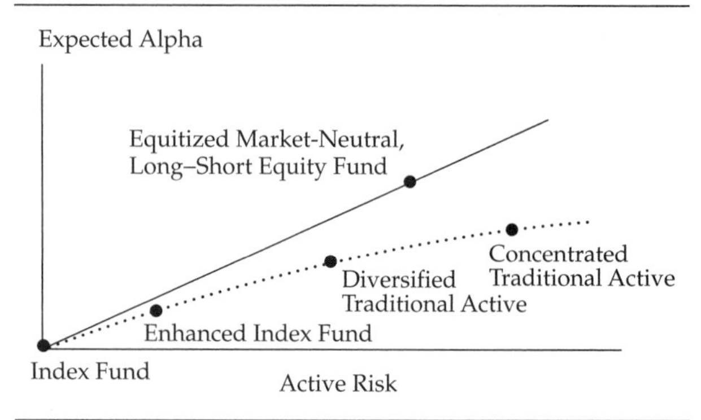

Note: Expected alpha is conditional on the manager having skill.

Source: Barclays Global Investors.

Manager structure optimization shows that if an investor seeks alpha and is averse to active risk, the weight in traditional active managers—especially those that are concentrated—should be greatly reduced. This result comes about because the no-shorting constraint hurts the IR of traditional, high-active-risk managers more than it does low-active-risk managers, such as enhanced index funds. (With the horizontal axis representing active risk and the vertical axis representing expected alpha, the IR is thus represented by the slope of the line at any given point.)

That the no-shorting constraint hurts higher-active-risk managers more than low-active-risk managers requires some explanation. All managers gather information about overpriced securities, which could be used to sell securities short. If a given manager cannot sell short, the manager can still choose not to own something that is in his or her benchmark. The more securities in the portfolio, the more opportunities to take advantage of the information that would otherwise cause a manager to short a stock. Managers who have a high-active-risk portfolio have far fewer holdings and thus far fewer opportunities to take advantage of any information about overpriced stocks. Thus, the IR is lower for these managers.

Investors who are allowed to sell short can choose from the portfolios on either line in Figure 1. If an investor has a high-active-risk budget, the investor's choices might include an equitized market-neutral, long–short hedge fund. Most of the rest of the portfolio would consist of enhanced index funds, with possibly a small allocation to traditional active funds that have particularly high expected alphas. An investor with a high-active-risk budget might not have any pure index funds in his or her optimum portfolio because index funds do not have enough active risk.

At a lower-active-risk budget, an investor who is allowed to sell short would build the portfolio out of index funds and enhanced index funds, plus potentially some of the equitized market-neutral, long–short hedge fund. Such an investor might also hold just a dollop of traditional active managers. Note that this entire analysis has been conducted as if the fees on the long–short and the long-only portfolios were the same. They are not. Investors have to calculate returns after costs, and long–short portfolios are quite aggressively priced these days.

Do Hedge Funds Charge Alpha Fees for Beta Performance?

My discussion of pure active risk and return can be applied to hedge funds and other alternative investments. Foremost, keep in mind that hedge fund managers are just active managers. There is no magic. The idea that a hedge fund manager is a crazed genius who allows a few of his wealthy friends to invest in the fund if they pay 2 percent of assets and 20 percent of the profit is obsolete. Such fee levels are ridiculous for hedge funds that are large institutional investment organizations. The 2 and 20 fee structure that makes perfect sense for the genius and his friends has been scaled up, without any discounting, to apply to investments in the billions of dollars for prominent hedge funds. The hedge fund fee structure has become little more than a mechanism for transferring wealth from the investor to the manager in a way that is not possible in a traditional, long-only portfolio where the fees and the strategies are more transparent.

Separating Alpha and Beta for Hedge Funds. Putting costs aside for the moment, I will discuss how an investor might apply to hedge funds my earlier comment that the dimensions of active management are pure active return, pure active risk, and costs.

The pure active return is the return left over after adjusting for any beta exposures that exist within the hedge fund. Many investors are used to thinking of beta as exposure to the stock market. But a whole array of other systematic risk factors can also be considered beta. In a meeting of the Foundation Financial Officers Group in Chicago in October 2003, Clifford Asness said that if a strategy can be written down, in the sense of a recipe that anyone can follow, it is passive and it is beta; anything else is alpha.

Following is a short list of potentially nonobvious beta exposures that are often found in hedge funds:

- value minus growth,
- duration (interest rate risk),
- credit spreads,
- optionality (e.g., being "short volatility"),
- buying merger targets, shorting the acquirers,
- buying convertible bonds, shorting the stock of the issuer,
- borrowing short, lending long when the yield curve is steep (carry trade), and
- borrowing in one currency, lending in another (international carry trade).

Clearly, a lot of market-type exposures are inherent in hedge fund strategies. Although index funds may not exist for these market factors, the systematic strategy can be identified and written down. In principle, investors are paying 2 and 20 for a package deal that includes both true alpha, which is the return above and beyond any returns from these systematic strategies, and a significant beta component. Getting 2 and 20 for the index part is nice work if a manager can get it.

Clifford Asness said something else very clever at the Chicago meeting: Alpha *becomes* beta over time once the source is discovered and promulgated. What is he talking about? Well, the first person to discover the return potential of value minus growth should be insulted to hear it called a beta factor because that person could have made a huge amount of money and nobody would have been able to determine where it was coming from. But now that everybody knows about it, it is beta. Not only can it be written down; it can be bought at very low cost using index funds or ETFs. Thus, to deserve the 2 and 20 fee structure, the hedge fund must be able to add alpha beyond merely being long in value and short in growth. Hence, alpha became beta over time.

I am not completely comfortable classifying anything that can be written down as beta. I think investors need to be able to "buy" a market factor through long and/or short positions in index funds, ETFs, futures, options, or swaps for it to be beta. Sometimes, investors have to pay alpha-like fees for exotic betas that are not yet available through lower-cost vehicles. I suspect that much of the success and popularity of hedge funds comes from their ability to sell exotic beta rather than from pure alpha as Asness stringently defines it.

Identifying Hedge Fund Betas: A Study. Bridgewater Associates conducted a wonderful study that sought to differentiate alpha from beta for hedge funds. Results for fixed-income arbitrage hedge funds are shown in **Figure 2**.

The dotted line represents six-month rolling returns of an index of fixed-income arbitrage hedge funds. The solid line is a model that Bridgewater devised that fits the managers' performance pretty closely. The alpha is the area created by geometrically subtracting the dotted line from the solid line. Beta is the extent to which the two lines zig and zag together. So, this figure presents a sort of visual returns-based style analysis. The correlation of the model with the managers is 59 percent, which is

Figure 2. Fixed-Income Arbitrage Six-Month Rolling Returns, June 1990–June 2003

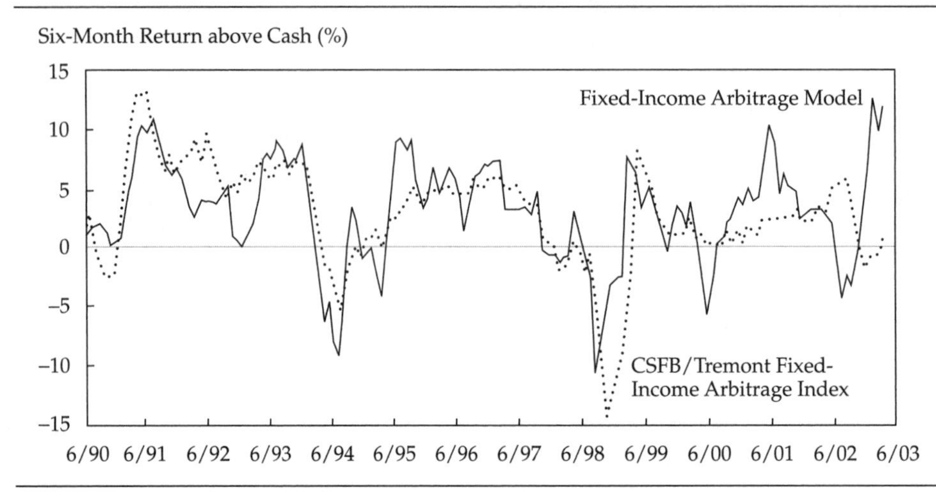

Note: The fixed-income arbitrage model consists of a 15 percent weight in the Eurodollar over Treasury spread, 5 percent in the emerging market debt spread over comparable-maturity U.S. Treasuries, 35 percent in the U.S. corporate bond spread over Treasuries, and 50 percent in the U.S. mortgage spread over Treasuries.

Source: Based on data from Bridgewater Associates.

pretty good considering that the managers typically claim they are absolute-return managers with no beta exposures. The important thing to note about this figure is how little space is between the dotted line and the solid line. In other words, these hedge fund managers produced very little alpha.

The results for emerging market hedge funds are shown in **Figure 3**. For this strategy, the Bridgewater model had a remarkable correlation of 81 percent, which corresponds to an R^2 of 65 percent. That is, 65 percent of the variation in these supposedly beta-free funds was explained by beta factors. Again, there is very little space between the solid line and the dotted line. There is a little alpha, but not very much.

Managed futures fund results are shown in **Figure 4**. The model had a correlation of 75 percent and, once again, a very high R^2. The model spends a significant amount of time ahead of the average manager.

Figure 3. Emerging Market Six-Month Rolling Returns, June 1990–June 2003

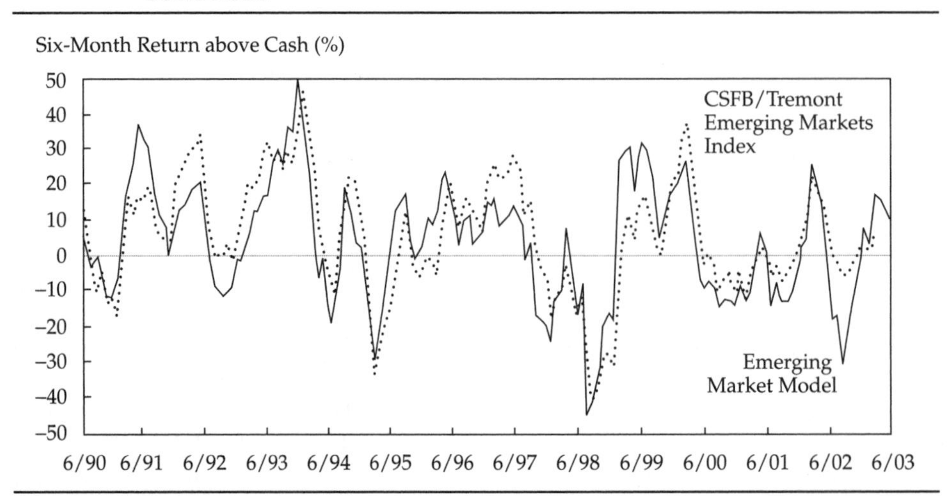

Note: The emerging market model is an equally weighted combination of emerging market debt and emerging market equity indexes.

Source: Based on data from Bridgewater Associates.

Figure 4. Managed Futures Six-Month Rolling Returns, July 1996–July 2003

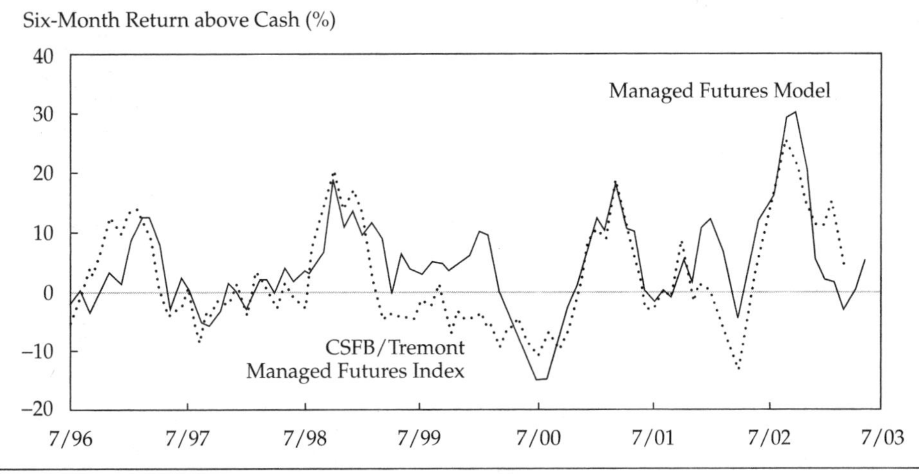

Notes: The managed futures model consists of a "1 × 3 month" momentum strategy in which one buys a given market if the one-month moving average is above the three-month moving average or sells if below. This strategy is followed on an equal-weighted basis across each of the following markets: the euro, yen, U.S. 10-year Treasury bond, S&P 500, and Eurodollar six-month maturity return above cash.

Source: Based on data from Bridgewater Associates.

In this case, it appears that active management subtracted alpha. The model consisted of a series of momentum trades, but one could build an index fund using these trades if so desired, although I do not think any such index funds currently exist.

Finally, merger arbitrage fund results are shown in **Figure 5**. The model was just the return on the S&P 500 Index, with an adjustment made for the number of merger and acquisition deals that were available to invest in. Considering how simple the model is, the tracking between it and the hedge funds' returns is fairly high, with a correlation of 52 percent. But the area between the solid line and the dotted line is substantial. Active managers made a lot more money than would have been achieved by investing in the model.

Figure 5. Merger Arbitrage Six-Month Rolling Returns, June 1990–June 2003

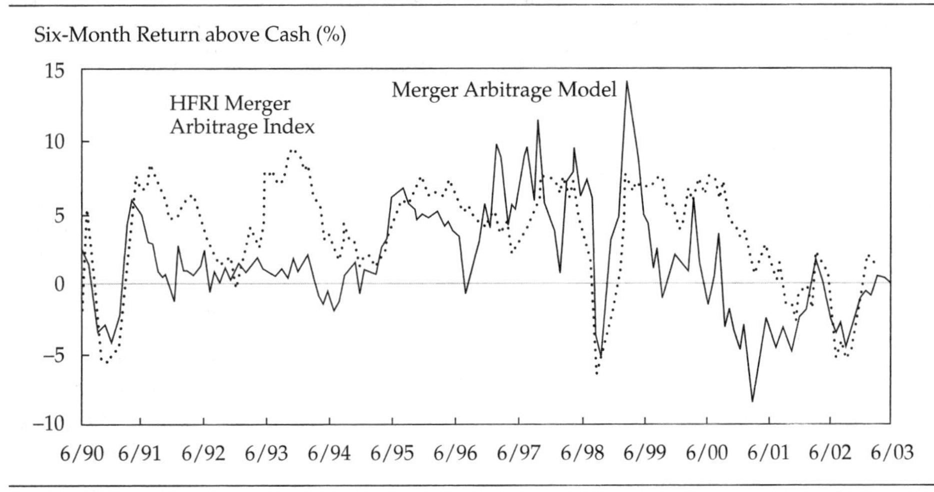

Note: The merger arbitrage model uses the six-month return above cash of the S&P 500, multiplied by a beta (between zero and one) proportional to the number of merger deals available in the market at each point in time.

Source: Based on data from Bridgewater Associates.

Policy Implications for Pension Funds and Other Investors

Every pool of assets has been accumulated for some reason. Usually, the assets exist to pay for an actual contracted liability or for a conceptual liability, such as retirement. Fortunately, people are catching on to the idea that the liability is really the ultimate benchmark. If an individual earns a return on his or her accumulated savings that is high enough to maintain his or her lifestyle in retirement, or if a plan sponsor is fully funded relative to its economically determined pension liability, or if the Ford Foundation earns a rate of return high enough to make the grants that it was established to make, then all three have achieved their investment goals.

Foundations. At the Ford Foundation, we have only one problem with that definition of success. Our liability (we are required to pay out annually 5.3 percent of whatever our asset value is at the time) makes us absolute-return investors in principle. But we do not know how to develop an asset allocation policy that has an expected return of 5.3 percent plus the inflation rate (to keep the purchasing power of the portfolio whole). We have to build the policy portfolio out of asset classes that exist. Our estimate for the expected real return on stocks is about 5 percent. Nominal bonds, TIPS (the common name for U.S. Treasury Inflation-Indexed Securities), real estate, cash, and other assets have even lower expected returns. Truly hedged hedge funds, if we held them, would have a zero beta and, for the purpose of calculating their expected return, the benchmark should be the return on cash. Of course, if we thought these funds were going to only earn the cash return, we would not buy them; we would hold cash instead. But any return offered by hedge funds beyond the return on the cash benchmark is alpha, and one should never put alpha into the expected return on a benchmark or policy portfolio. The policy portfolio should consist only of betas, and the production of alpha can then be measured relative to this purely beta-driven benchmark.

So, to answer the question of whether there should be a policy portfolio for an institution with an absolute-return payout requirement, the answer is that we do need one, and it should be built out of assets for which index funds exist. Ours happens to be constructed from indexes of U.S. and international equities, nominal bonds, TIPS, and cash. We can then judge the success of our active asset allocation decisions by reference to this policy portfolio. Of course, we can change the policy portfolio when we believe it is prudent to do so. There is no reason that it should be static, although changing it all the time would tend to blur the distinction between active and policy decisions.

We can also compare our performance with that of a hypothetical asset that returns 5.3 percent plus the inflation rate. But if we decide that we are unable to add alpha, we cannot index the portfolio instead and earn this rate of return. That is why an absolute-return benchmark does not make a lot of sense.

Defined-Benefit Pension Plans. Defined-benefit pension plans have a special set of challenges because the size of the liabilities is set in a process that has nothing to do with the size of the assets. Although a foundation's liabilities are linked to the assets by a simple formula, in a pension plan, the liabilities are set by contracting with the workers without reference to what assets may be available to pay the pension benefits. It is then the sponsor's problem to accumulate enough assets through a mix of pension contributions and investment returns.

To minimize required contributions from the sponsor, many pension plans have adopted very high equity allocations, 70 percent or more. But such an allocation creates a great deal of risk in the pension plan because the pension liabilities look more like a portfolio of nominal bonds and TIPS with only a little in equities. Pension plans should thus consider lowering their equity allocations.

Looked at another way, a pension plan is just a project of the sponsoring corporation. If investing in the S&P 500 is such a great proposition, why not shut down the factory, sell the assets, and just buy shares of the S&P 500 to increase the productivity of the company's capital? The fact that no company ever does that shows companies do not think investing in the S&P 500 is such a great corporate project.

Some people wonder whether a broad shift among pension plans toward a closer match of assets and liabilities would cause the market to decline. If all pension funds decided at once that they needed to sell equities and get to a position that more closely matched their liabilities, who would be buying the equities? The answer is that the investors who hold the shares in these corporations would suddenly find out that they are short in beta because the companies themselves in which they hold stock no longer have a leveraged position in the S&P 500. So, to keep their risk level the same and the reward for taking the risk the same, they would have to buy the equities that the pension funds would be selling. In the short run, any change in the supply and demand for an asset produces volatility. But in the long run, it would not change the overall price level of the market.

Stated another way, if companies that have a bet on the S&P 500 in their pension funds are currently fairly priced and they then unwind this bet, the risk of the companies must go down but not the expected return, so the stocks will be self-evidently a bargain and investors will buy them.

Defined-Contribution Plans and Individual Investing. The defined-contribution world, which is a subset of individual investing, has been poorly served by the financial system because it sells plan participants high-cost products that produce negative alpha, on average, even before fees. Furthermore, investors do not understand the efficient frontier or how to build an optimal portfolio. Every worker—every airline pilot, every nurse, and every tort lawyer—has gotten roped into the position of being a chief investment officer for his or her own assets.

These workers never asked for this responsibility and have never claimed they were good at it; by and large, they are not. Why not just do it for them? If they could invest in a well-engineered, optimized portfolio consisting mostly of index funds but with some active funds mixed in that are carefully chosen by the sponsor, they would have a lot more money for their retirement and they would be earning it with a lot less risk. In other words, we should be working hard to try to get the principles that I just discussed, which are gaining currency in the world of institutional investing, applied to individuals' investments too.

Question and Answer Session

Laurence B. Siegel

Question: If employees do not require extra compensation for having underfunded pensions, then such underfunded pensions represent free debt. Do employees require such compensation?

Siegel: If employees become involuntary lenders to the company by having a pension plan that is underfunded and thus have to worry about whether they're going to get their pensions, they should in theory be able to negotiate for higher wages because the company is cheating them out of something they have agreed to be paid. In practice, I don't think that they are able to do anything of the kind.

Generally, companies with underfunded plans are poorly managed in other ways as well. Employees of these companies would often be better off looking for another job. But having given up something without any compensation, the employees should either attempt to negotiate a higher wage or get the company to fully fund the plan, which is a much cheaper solution to the same problem. In fact, it is free. The company doesn't give up anything by fully funding the plan because it owes the money anyway, but the employees get something, which is the reduced risk that they will not be paid their pension.

Question: Are endowments that have invested heavily in hedge funds earning alpha?

Siegel: I think the early adopters earned a lot of alpha. But now that the number of hedge funds has ballooned to 6,000, there is the danger that high compensation schemes have attracted low-skilled people as well as the smartest people. The fees are so high that a lot of "dumb but lucky" managers are going to earn high compensation while the process of weeding out the good from the bad takes place. I'm willing to bet that not nearly as many people will earn alpha from hedge funds going forward.

Question: Is it true that all investors cannot hire index managers because indexing cannot exist without a large component of the market being active?

Siegel: I've been hearing this argument since I was a student. Every time a professor would bring up the efficient market hypothesis, a smart kid in the front row would put up her hand and say that if everybody indexed, the market wouldn't be efficient and prices would be unrelated to value because nobody would be analyzing securities. Roger Ibbotson calls this the "student's proof" of market inefficiency, and it is right.

I don't know whether it takes 10 percent or 80 percent of all investments to be indexed for prices to be unrelated to value. It seems that in every generation there is some kind of bubble or depression where stock prices are unrelated to value, either on the up side or the down side, at least in some industries. We have just been through such a period. So, at the very least, indexing has not made the market self-evidently *more* efficient.

But I think we are very far from a point where indexing is so pervasive that it makes successful active management easy. Most active managers underperform their benchmarks, and you would have done better to invest in an index fund.

Question: What are some of the qualitative elements you should consider when estimating manager alpha and tracking error?

Siegel: We'd look to see whether the historical track record was superior on a properly risk-adjusted basis. But we also want to deal with sensible and reputable people from whom we can learn something. When you talk to a lot of smart people, everybody seems pretty good. But then you have to remember that they're all betting against each other, which is how they're trying to earn alpha. So, you have to look for somebody who is truly superior even in that population.

Thus, I'm looking for somebody who can teach me something original and different, distinguishing himself or herself from the rest of this population that has already been weeded out pretty well.

Question: If the roughly eight defined strategies in Tremont Advisers' hedge fund indexes are different beta strategies, then should we be combining the ones with less than perfectly correlated betas with stocks, bonds, and cash?

Siegel: Yes. That is one of the hidden implications of the principles that I have just explained. Once we've built a portfolio of stocks, bonds, and cash betas, we need to see if we can find some other betas that are not perfectly correlated with these and that have a payoff. To the extent we can, it raises the efficient frontier.

The hedge fund strategies that I discussed show some pretty strong evidence that they had a payoff over some reasonably long period. So, I would say "yes," but not at any price. Hedge fund investors should be cognizant of high fees, which raise the performance hurdle. If there is a way to get exotic beta without paying alpha fees, and if exotic beta and not pure alpha is what you want, you should do so.

Question: How do you incorporate fees into your portfolio optimizations?

Siegel: We would subtract the expected fees from the expected alpha. Note that I said "expected" fees, because the fees are typically conditional on the production of alpha; thus, it is not trivial to estimate them.

Question: Most corporate pension funds and Treasury departments are not abandoning current or even loss-making operations to invest in equities. Is it because they lack an understanding of alpha, of equities, and of the true potential of professional investment management? Or, is it because most executives are personally not successful investors?

Siegel: I think it is because they have a mandate to try to make a go of their auto company, gas company, or software company and not turn their operations into a mutual fund. If they did, shareholders would find another CEO. Shareholders who want to invest in the stock market can do so on their own.

Question: If one accepts the forecast that stocks and bonds will have disappointing returns over the next 20 years, is a long–short strategy a better proxy for equity exposure inclusive of alpha and beta for managing downside drawdowns on an absolute-return basis?

Siegel: There are two things you can do: Live with the low returns, or aggressively add alpha knowing that your chance of succeeding is probably 50 percent. We all want to add alpha, but there should be a backup plan for living with lower returns.

Question: If a manager beats an index by timing weights of high- and low-beta stocks, is that not a source of alpha?

Siegel: Excess return that is created by timing between different beta exposures will show up as alpha in a proper analysis and should be compensated as such.

Question: How predictive is the past record of good managers?

Siegel: It is much less accurate than I would like, but it is not useless. Good performance tends to be predictive for a while because of a momentum effect. If there is a group of stocks that has moved up, all of a sudden everybody wants to buy those stocks. Money then flows into the funds, forcing them to buy more of the same stocks. So, managers can ride that wave a little bit, but that isn't real skill. Fortunately, real skill is also somewhat predictable, but with a wide forecast error.

The Changing Role of the Policy Portfolio

Martin L. Leibowitz
Vice Chairman and Chief Investment Officer
TIAA-CREF
New York City

The policy portfolio has traditionally been thought of as a static entity; that is, once established, it does not change. But recent market moves and investor behavior patterns have called into question the rigidity of the policy portfolio. The potential solution is a more fluid, adaptive policy portfolio that is responsive to discernible changes in the market.

At AIMR's 2003 Annual Conference, Peter Bernstein gave a presentation in which he called into question the typical approach for handling the policy portfolio.[1] Since that time, I have been reconsidering the conventional wisdom surrounding the policy portfolio. This presentation is thus my reflections on what the policy portfolio was, is, and could be.

One View of the Policy Portfolio

Traditionally, as shown in **Figure 1**, the policy portfolio is constructed by evaluating prospects for market returns while simultaneously considering the sponsor's asset/liability situation and risk tolerance, which are influenced by multiple considerations. The benefit of having a policy portfolio is that it represents a pragmatic way of articulating the best discernible balance among the sponsor's risk tolerance, asset/liability situation, and long- and short-term market prospects . . . at a particular point in time. Thus, someone who is fundamentally in charge, someone who is essentially the agent of the ultimate beneficiary of these investments, determines the asset allocation, the policy, for the assets. The investment manager is then asked to implement this policy and told that he or she has some flexibility in implementation and, therefore, can take some risks but only to the extent described in the policy. It is thus a sharing of understanding and of communication around the policy portfolio goals and objectives; it is an acknowledgment of the investment committee, or whatever entity is the beneficiary's representative, taking responsibility. But importantly, it is at a particular point in time.

The real issue is that a static policy portfolio cannot be responsive to changes in a sponsor's risk tolerance, changes in the asset/liability situation, and/or *discernible* changes in long- or short-term market prospects. And note that I am saying that a sponsor's risk tolerance does change. It may change for internal reasons that have nothing to do with the market, but the risk tolerance may also change as a by-product of market events. For example, the market takes a big tumble and the sponsor finds itself in a position where it is getting harder pressed to meet its imminent liabilities, or even its longer-term liabilities if its funding ratio decreases to a danger point. In this case, this sponsor's risk should be responsive and, therefore, should change.

The word "discernible" is important in the aforementioned description. The market may change and the prospects may change, but if those changes are not discernible, there is no basis for taking action and the sponsor thus sticks with the portfolio it has. Most institutions, at least in the shorter and intermediate terms, tend to rebalance back to a policy portfolio.

Therefore, because the ingredients that determine the policy portfolio are subject to change, what is needed is a more adaptive (not a static) policy portfolio. Why, one might ask, is this issue coming

[1] For a printed version of this talk see Peter L. Bernstein, "Points of Inflection: Investment Management Tomorrow," *Financial Analysts Journal* (July/August 2003): 18–23.

Editor's Note: Martin L. Leibowitz recently retired as vice chairman and chief investment officer at TIAA-CREF (Teachers Insurance and Annuity Association-College Retirement Equities Fund) and has become managing director in the research department of Morgan Stanley.

Figure 1. Traditional Policy Portfolio

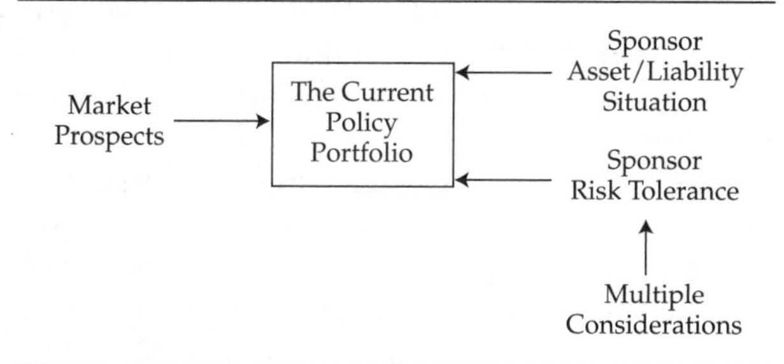

up now? My answer is that the famous words "this time it is different" may really be true. Some fundamental changes are going on in the marketplace in terms of how investors look at investments. Some of these changes have been sparked by the work that Robert Arnott, Clifford Asness, and Peter Bernstein have done in regards to the existence of a low equity risk premium in the market today.[2] If investors believe that the risk premium is low, discernibly low, that belief implies a change in the standard way of looking at investments, and not just at this point in time. It suggests that investors can see changes in the risk premium over the course of time and that these changes may be discernible and actionable.

Thus, what I am arguing for is an adaptive policy portfolio. My basic contention is that a more fluid, adaptive policy portfolio with a higher level of plasticity has become more appropriate in light of current times and most likely future trends.

Deinstitutionalization: Rise of DC Plans

The rise of defined-contribution (DC) plans and IRAs as a primary mode of preparing for retirement is one of the fundamental changes in the marketplace that is motivating the move toward an adaptive policy portfolio. The total U.S. retirement market is shown in **Figure 2**. Its peak was near $12 trillion in the late 1990s, and thus, the retirement market is a large percentage of the overall U.S. financial market.

Some of the ingredients of the total retirement market are shown in **Figure 3**. The line for the IRA market mostly reflects rollover IRAs. These are not IRAs where investors put their annual contributions of $3,000. These are IRAs for people who left their companies and who needed to roll the balance of their 401(k)s into another vehicle. Rollover IRAs are by far the fastest growing component of the IRA market.

[2]See Robert D. Arnott and Peter L. Bernstein, "What Risk Premium Is 'Normal'?" *Financial Analysts Journal* (March/April 2002):64–85, and Clifford S. Asness, "Stocks versus Bonds: Explaining the Equity Risk Premium," *Financial Analysts Journal* (March/April 2000):96–113.

Figure 2. Total U.S. Retirement Market, 1990–2002

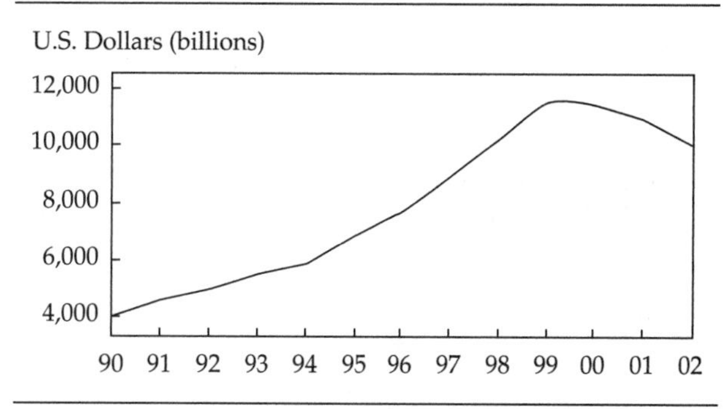

Sources: Based on data from the Investment Company Institute, Federal Reserve, American Council of Life Insurers, and IRS.

Figure 3. DC and IRA Plans, 1990–2002

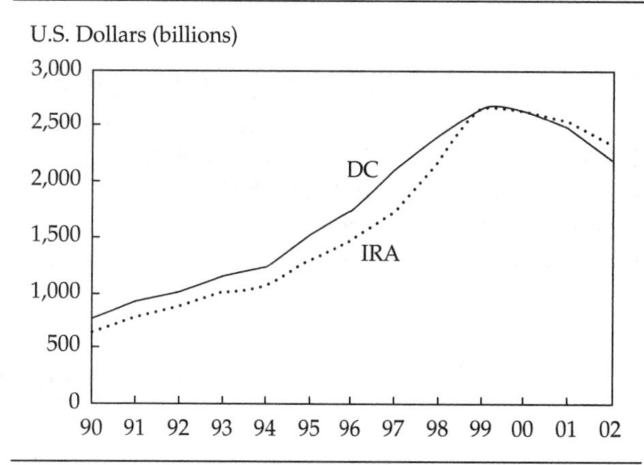

Sources: Based on data from the Investment Company Institute, Henry McVey (Morgan Stanley), Federal Reserve, American Council of Life Insurers, and IRS.

Figure 4 is another perspective of the retirement market. It compares public plans and private defined-benefit (DB) plans with DC plans and IRAs. As shown in the figure, the combination of DC plans and IRAs has surpassed the combination of public plans and private DB plans and should continue to do so. The result of this change is an increasing reliance on individual decisions and individual controlled assets. Interestingly, for the most part, workers prefer DC plans because they can see that the money is there and know that it is not subject to their future with the company. Corporations prefer DC plans for a lot of reasons, including the fact that they typically cost an awful lot less than DB plans. So, it looks like everyone wins with DC plans, which unfortunately, as basic economics suggests, is not quite true. I will expand on this important notion further in the next section.

Figure 4. Total DC vs. Total DB Plans, 1990–2002

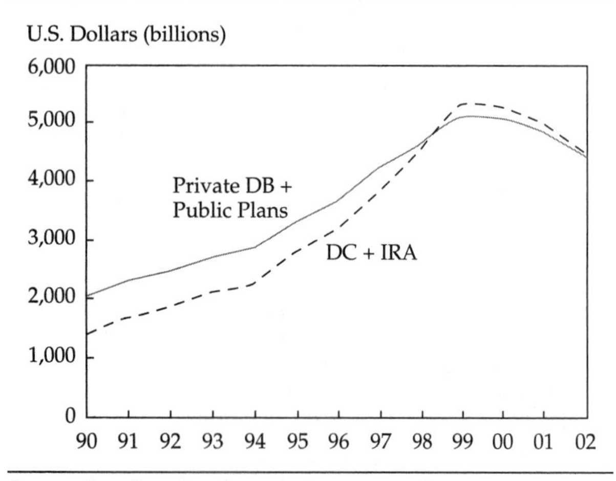

Sources: Based on data from the Investment Company Institute, Federal Reserve, American Council of Life Insurers, and IRS.

Different Rebalancing Strategies

At the beginning of 2003, one of my colleagues at the Teachers Insurance and Annuity Association-College Retirement Equities Fund (TIAA-CREF), Brett Hammond, and I became curious about how participants rebalance in the face of market moves. Clearly, some radical market moves had occurred in the previous couple of years, with a few billion dollars sloshing around here and there. The question we posed to ourselves was: What does the rebalancing look like in aggregate?

Figure 5 shows the behavior of our participants at TIAA-CREF as well as that of endowments. Note that this figure represents just equity and fixed-income-related accounts; other accounts were removed. Thus, individuals had 60 percent of their portfolios in equities in June 1997. We then calculated what the equity allocation would have been if participants had not rebalanced and had, therefore, just stuck with that beginning allocation as the market moved. The result is shown by the light gray lines, and the outcome was roughly a 65 percent allocation to equities by December 1998. The dotted line shows the actual equity allocations through time. Thus, as can be seen from this graph, in any particular year, it was the market movement that ultimately determined the ending allocation of our participants in aggregate. The same pattern of the two allocations being different by just a couple of percentage points held for the entire sample period, even when the market was on its way down and then back up.

Figure 5. Actual and Projected Equity Allocations, June 1997–December 2003

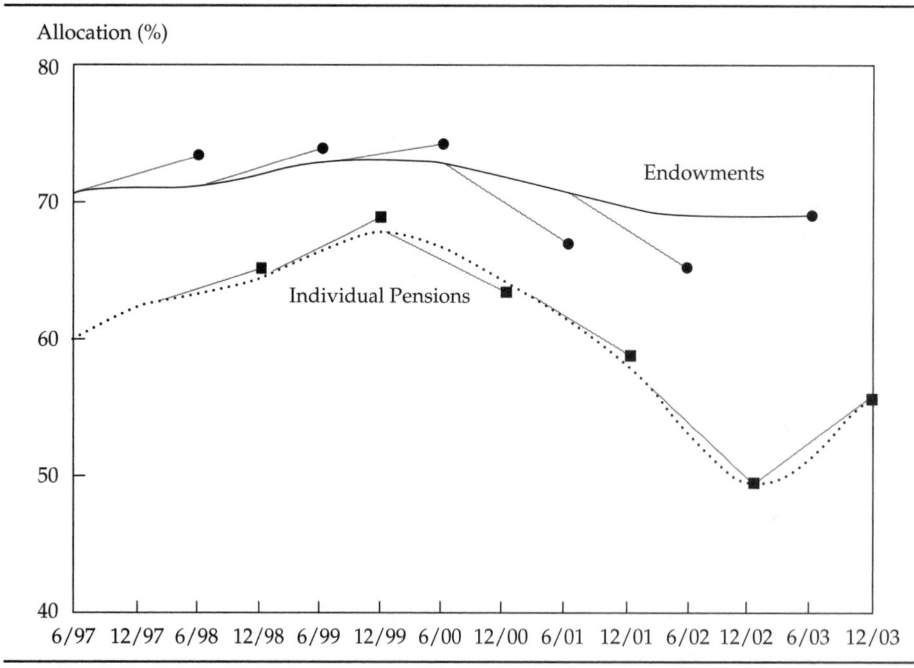

Note: This figure represents only equity and fixed-income accounts; other accounts were removed from the data.

Sources: Based on data on individual pensions (TIAA-CREF) and college endowments (TIAA-CREF and National Association of College and University Business Officers survey).

We also conducted the same allocation analysis with endowments. Endowments' fiscal years are mid-year, so in June 1997, they had an equity allocation of roughly 71 percent. If they had stuck with that allocation, in June 1998, the equity allocation would have been about 73 percent. In reality, they ended up still at about 71 percent. This difference is even more dramatic during the market decline. If they had stuck with their allocations in 1999, they would have gone from 73 percent all the way down to 66 percent by fiscal year-end 2000, but they ended up basically at 71 percent. That is, they fundamentally rebalanced. The real message then from this figure is that endowments rebalance, and individuals do not.

This analysis led us to the next question: Can we categorize how/why people rebalance? We concluded with the following categorization of rebalancing behaviors:

- rebalancers,
- holders,
- shifters, and
- valuators.

The first two categories basically reflect rather formulaic responses to market moves, either no response or a response to move back to the original allocation. A shift, however, is a movement in allocation that is based on the internal needs, views, and tolerances of the organization itself. It is not driven primarily by the market per se or a view of market prospects, although a shift can be secondarily driven by the market. Suppose, for example, that the market takes a huge tumble and a plan finds its funding ratio is down from 120 percent to 80 percent. That new funding ratio may be the basis for making a change, but the change is not a result of a change in the sponsor's view of the market. The change occurs because the sponsor's situation has changed. The last category, valuators, are those who are making changes because they think that the market has changed in terms of either its return or risk prospects.

The following scenario provides an example of these four allocator types. A rebalancer starts off with a 60 percent equity allocation, the market drops 20 percent (although, interestingly, the equity allocation drops only 5 percent), and the rebalancer moves the portfolio back to a 60 percent allocation very quickly. A holder in the same situation similarly sees the market push his allocation down to 55 percent, but he stays at 55 percent.

A valuator also starts at 60 percent and sees that the market has pushed the allocation down to 55 percent. The valuator could thus have two points of view. First, with a contrarian view, the valuator would take the allocation beyond the original 60 percent level (i.e., with the belief that the market is now cheap, a 70 percent allocation may seem appropriate). Second, with a momentum view, the valuator might want to get out of this market environment and take the allocation down to 40 percent. One cannot predict how valuators—in aggregate—will behave.

A shifter can go also in either direction. But generally, if a market move puts a shifter in a situation where the assets shrink relative to the liabilities, the shifter is likely to take less risk, although one certainly can envision other reactions.

We then looked at various institutional categories to see where their behavior patterns fall. The results, based somewhat on speculation, are shown in **Exhibit 1**. DC plans and IRAs tend to fall into the holder category. In spite of the market actions of the past few years, they basically held, although they could potentially become shifters at some point. Institutional investors, for the most part, would claim to be rebalancers. So, who are the valuators? The answer is hedge funds and even more strongly foreign investors and traders. Interestingly, almost anyone could be a shifter if the portfolio comes under sufficient stress.

Exhibit 1. Institutional Categories and Behavior Patterns

Institutional Category	Rebalancers	Holders	Shifters	Valuators
DB pensions	XX		X	
Endowments/ foundations	XX		X	
DC pensions/IRAs		XX	X	
Mutual funds		XX	X	
Foreign investors	X	X	X	XX
Hedge funds	XX			X
Traders				XX

The effects on the market from these various behavior patterns can be seen in **Exhibit 2**. Holders basically have no effect on the market. They are neither buyers nor sellers. Rebalancers are smoothers. The market goes up, and they sell to bring their allocation down. The market goes down, and they buy to bring it back up. Valuators can also be smoothers, to the extent that they are contrarians.

So, the real question is: Who are the exacerbaters? Who has the potential to create an adverse feedback mechanism in the market? The market goes

Exhibit 2. Behavior Patterns and Market Impact

Market Impact	Rebalancers	Holders	Shifters	Valuators
Neutral		XX		
Smoothing	XX		X	XX
Exacerbating		X	XX	X

down, and it hurts so much that they want to actually unload; they want to sell. Well, certainly, a participant who can become a shifter when under sufficient stress is likely to be a seller in a bad market. For example, holders may find themselves outside some comfort band and thus move into an exacerbating mode. And valuators can go either way—either smooth or exacerbate market moves.

One way of looking at the whole process of portfolio revision is to start off with the current portfolio, whether it is called a policy portfolio or not, and based on market moves see what is going to happen, as shown in **Figure 6**. Faced with a market move, a rebalancer will just go back to the original allocation, almost unthinkingly, or at least it appears that way. A holder will simply stick with the ending portfolio. A valuator will take a look at the market move and at how the market has changed in terms of its risk–return characteristics and then go through a process of deciding whether making a move one way or the other is worthwhile. The shifter has not necessarily changed his view of the market, but the move itself may have altered his own situation, which is the key. For example, he may find that he has some new needs that he did not expect to have or that he is closer to his liability payouts. Thus, based on these changes (and not his view of the market), he may find himself reassessing his risk tolerance—deciding on a new allocation and seeing if it is sufficiently different to justify the transaction costs of rebalancing. The shifter, therefore, is fundamentally different from these other three categories.

Risk Tolerance and the Shifter

At this point, I want to delve into the risk tolerance aspect of the shifter. And thinking in terms of two different forms of risk tolerance is useful in this setting. The first form is what I would call "objective risk tolerance," and the second is the emotional overlay, what I call the "20 percent rule."

Objective Risk Tolerance Factors. What kinds of considerations go into determining the objective risk tolerance? A totally rational economic being would consider the following:

- nature of liabilities,
- asset/liability surplus cushion,
- pattern of future contributions,
- liability horizon (e.g., payouts that are coming due 20 years from now create a very different need from the payouts that have to be funded next year),
- interest rate structure at horizon,
- liability flexibility,
- liability uncertainty,
- prospect of contingencies, and
- contribution flexibility.

Organizational considerations also need to be considered. For example, what is the nature of the backup resources that exist? If an investor has a rich uncle (and the uncle likes the investor), that is a very different situation from one where an investor has only herself to rely on. For a DB plan, a strong corporate sponsor could serve as a backup resource.

Figure 6. An Idealized Portfolio Revision Process

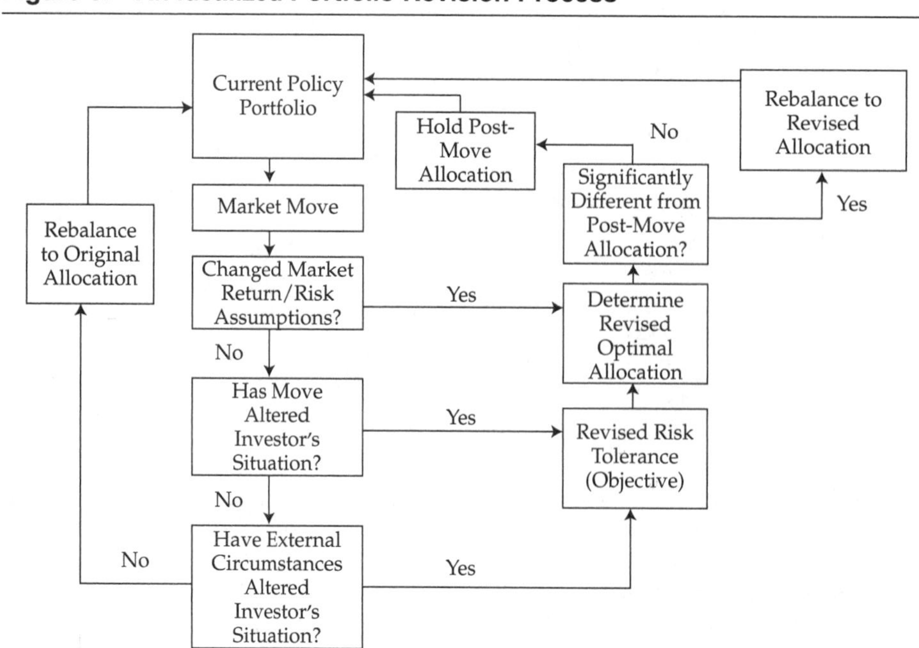

Another factor is the feedback from the rebalancing strategy. If you are an investor who is never going to rebalance, that says something about the level of risk that you can take. Liquidity and regulatory considerations are also important in terms of the kinds of risks investors take. Scale of assets is another factor to consider, as is the intensity of monitoring and subsequent actionability. An investor who is willing to take actions continuously has a different risk tolerance from one whose investment committee addresses risk issues on a biannual basis.

Figure 7 shows the effect of risk tolerance/asset allocation on a change in the market. If an investor's portfolio is at the "current market" point and the market moves up, the surplus increases and the investor's ability to objectively take risk may well increase significantly. Similarly, if the market goes down, the investor's ability to objectively take risk may also go down because the cushion has eroded. Thus, an "S" curve characterizes individual investors' risk tolerance. Notice the distinction between individual and institutional risk tolerance. Individuals, especially those who have relatively modest backup resources or none at all, have to be more sensitive, objectively, to market movements. Institutions, generally speaking, have more flexibility because they typically have more assets, a longer time horizon, and more backup resources. So, institutions may be in a position where they can have a flatter curve and can maintain their risk tolerance through tougher circumstances.

Figure 7. Objective Risk Tolerance as a Function of Market Level

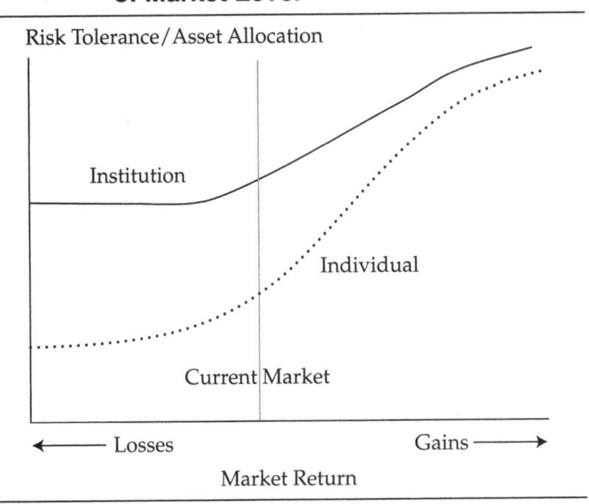

Emotional Overlay: The 20 Percent Rule. Because investors are not totally rational beings, emotion is a factor in risk tolerance analysis. I think of this emotional overlay as the "20 percent rule," which is a loose rule that I developed through my experience over the years. It suggests the following: Many investors think of themselves as long-term oriented and adopt long-term strategies. If I were to ask them what they would do if their overall portfolio (not just their equity component) dropped by 5 percent, they would answer: "I am taking a long-term view. What do you mean 5 percent? Of course I am going to see it through. I am not going to change anything." If I were to then ask about the effect of a 10 percent drop, I would hear: "A 10 percent loss is starting to be painful, but over the long term, I can tolerate that drop." At a 15 percent drop, they would pause. And at 20 percent, investors would confess that they would have to start some serious thinking about their situation. So, even truly long-term investors may change their perceptions following a 20 percent drop; hence, my 20 percent rule: A 20 percent drop represents sufficient pain for even long-term investors to consider short-term readjustments.

Figure 8 distinguishes between the objective and emotional risk tolerances for an individual investor. As can be seen from the dashed line for the emotional risk tolerance, holding behavior takes place in the ±20 percent portfolio change range; that is, no changes occur. When the loss is greater than 20 percent, however, shifting occurs. And in the particular case of *losses* greater than 20 percent, a more pronounced behavioral risk aversion results relative to like gains.

Market Implications

So, what are the market implications of these rebalancing behaviors? Certainly, corporate DB plans are not growing, although public DB plans are the one

Figure 8. Behavioral Risk Tolerance/Asset Allocation as a Function of Market Level

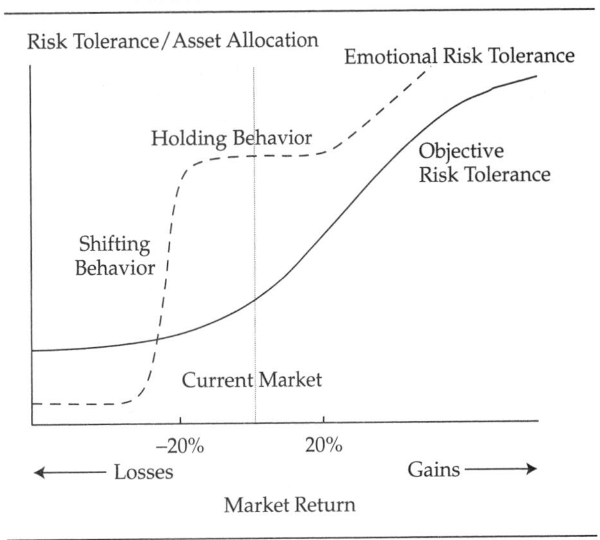

component of the DB market that is growing. Nonetheless, more and more retirement assets are moving into a DC format. As such, individuals are making the decisions about their asset allocation. One of the saddest issues in this context is the tax-deferred illusion: People think they have a lot more savings in their retirement accounts than they really do. The issue arises when these retirement savings are translated into a much lower after-tax, after-inflation stream of payments postretirement. I think the United States is facing a huge crisis in terms of people finding themselves with insufficient funds to carry them through retirement in a reasonable fashion, and sadly, I do not think that most investors are fully aware of this problem. We all seem to possess a strange discounting function. Things that are over the horizon seem like they are never going to happen, and only the things that are right in front of our noses do we take very, very seriously. So, this asset/liability deficit in the pension world will seem ever more visible as time progresses, which will inevitably create a greater emotional overlay. One could argue that the increasing visibility of this pension problem could create some greater market volatility, which could, in turn, create some unfortunate results. An advantage of an investor having steady hands is that when the market tumbles, the investor does not throw all his or her cards in the air. Institutions and committees tend to be a steadying hand, even in the face of tough times. Investors who have weak hands, however, can be whipsawed. They often buy or sell at exactly the wrong time.[3] So, one could envision a market that has a great deal of polarization between the institutions and the individuals, between the strong hands and the weak hands.

Asset Management Implications

One of the implications of this rebalancing behavior for asset management is greater volatility driven by higher emotional content, especially as a follow-on to extreme market movements. Another implication is more-radical changes in the risk premium, especially as investors see the market becoming cheaper or dearer at various points in time. And importantly, to the extent that those changes are driven by technical effects that are identifiable, the changes in the risk premium will have a greater level of discernibility. Discernibility is the key ingredient. If an investor can discern with some significant level of conviction that the risk premium has really changed, then that investor can react via changes in his or her asset allocation. The risk premium changes all the time, but only if it is discernible do more opportunities exist for policy portfolio revisions based on it. Notice, however, that I am not talking about trying to time the market day in and day out but, rather, about making opportunistic moves at discernible elbow points in the market. The final implication is that behavioral finance will play an increasing role at this macro level.

Adaptive Policy Portfolio

The result of my ruminations on the policy portfolio is a recommendation that we investment professionals start thinking in terms of an adaptive policy portfolio, one that changes not day by day but responds to discernible changes in the situation of the sponsoring entity as well as to evolving market opportunities. With such a policy portfolio, investors would need to ask themselves whether the risk–return assumptions have changed in a discernible fashion. If the answer is "yes," they would go through the whole process of revising the allocation. Such investors would be neither holders nor shifters nor rebalancers. They would be integrators of all the considerations shown in Figure 6.

In sum, my basic contention is that a more fluid, adaptive policy portfolio with a higher level of plasticity has become more appropriate in light of current times and future trends.

[3]See the Dalbar study Quantitative Analysis of Investor Behavior, which is updated yearly and can be accessed at www.dalbarinc.com/content/showpage.asp?page=2003071601&r=/pressroom/default.asp&s=Return+To+Press+Releases.

Question and Answer Session

Martin L. Leibowitz

Question: If a DB sponsor adopts a risk-budgeting approach, is there still a need for a policy portfolio?

Leibowitz: Yes. The issue of what overall risk and what type of risk the sponsor wants to take should be attuned to a policy portfolio that articulates those risks and that changes as the sponsor's situation changes.

Question: What are your thoughts on the recent flurry of principal-protected products?

Leibowitz: Asymmetric returns is a wonderful goal. The fundamental issue is to get it at a reasonable cost over time. For long-term plans to be asymmetrical in formal ways, however, is very costly.

In some ways, when you have an adaptive policy portfolio, you may be in essence creating a kind of asymmetry. If you find yourself in a situation where your asset/liability cushion has declined and you decide to reduce your risk, you're basically invoking a dynamic allocation process. In effect, you will be reducing your risk as the market declines, and as you find the market giving you a better cushion, you may take more risk if you deem that the risk is appropriate.

Question: When and how are changes in the risk premium discernible?

Leibowitz: A lot of people had a sense that the risk premium had indeed changed between 1995 and 2000, but for many reasons, including the mind-set of a static policy and a rigid rebalancing approach, few responded. Discernible doesn't mean it is easy, and it certainly doesn't mean that under normal circumstances you'll be able to make that determination with absolute certainty or on a day-by-day basis.

Question: Doesn't the introduction of a liability stream into the asset allocation decision make the Markowitz optimization framework obsolete as a static model?

Leibowitz: There are ways to create a balanced optimization that tries to achieve both liability and asset goals. The Markowitz approach can be readily extended to incorporate a surplus-optimization goal.

Question: How serious are your concerns about aggregate, societal, future retirement funding levels?

Leibowitz: I want to be a prophet of concern, not of doom. It is always easier to project out the problems that exist than to see the solutions that a creative and dynamic population can develop in response to them. It is an act of faith that all problems will one way or another be addressed and at least be resolved if not solved.

At the same time, we are well advised to look into the future to see where issues are serious and where problems confront us. The tax-deferred illusion discussed earlier is one such issue. People see a chunk of money that they had never seen before—$50,000 for some, $100,000 for others, $1 million for others. A lot of money is in some of these tax-deferred plans, but relative to individuals' lifestyles and relative to effective taxes, low interest rates, and inflation, it may not cover an even modest proportion of their needs.

Question: When does an adaptive policy change become market timing?

Leibowitz: When you're trying to be in the primary business of timing the market, that's timing. And that, as we've seen repeatedly, is a tough game to play on a daily basis. Making moves that respond to discernible changes in the market, which should not happen very often, is something that makes strategic sense. Deliberately or not, institutions and individual investors do it, so we might as well be up-front about it.

Question: Why is the notion of plasticity new to investment management?

Leibowitz: What has happened is that we have moved toward a business model where more and more practitioners focus on relative returns, and that model makes a lot of sense. But it has led to a situation where we have a fairly static relative-return way of looking at market silos without some of the fluidity that we had in the past.

What is new is that we are calling for a more deliberate adoption of flexibility, and we're also calling attention to the increasing role of individuals and how they may behave, especially in terms of their retirement funds.

Question: Please comment on the use of simulation for asset/liability studies.

Leibowitz: There are some really magnificent planning tools around that are now available to individuals virtually for nothing, such as Financial Engines.[1] These products are quite sophisticated and comprehensive, and they exceed what was available to institutions from the top consultants a few years ago.

[1]See www.financialengines.com.

These products do, however, need to be taken with a grain of salt. There is a danger that people take computer simulations as being too much of a science. And the final analysis is only as good as the underlying models and fundamental assumptions. This field is not a science, and it is important to convey the uncertainty of many of the basic assumptions that we have. In all that we do in this field, we must accept a significant and irreducible level of "model risk."

Question: Are endowments rebalancing between debt and equity, or are they moving into absolute-return strategies that offer better risk–reward ratios than traditional investments?

Leibowitz: More and more, endowments are moving some of their fixed-income component into absolute return, and they are moving some of their U.S. equity component into private equity types of formats. This movement into absolute return and private equity is more of a secular change than a rebalancing of portions of their fixed-income and equity components because of market moves.

Question: Does a lack of investment choices (even if it is done in an effort to avoid confusion) limit the ability of employees to invest properly in DC plans?

Leibowitz: The real issue is not so much how many choices are available but what is the market spectrum spanned. It is awfully nice to have a real estate alternative, and it would be nice to have a sanitized hedge fund alternative for individuals who might not otherwise be able to invest in hedge funds. That certainly is a consideration.

One of the problems is that so many of the fixed-income products have horrendous fees, and it is especially important for individuals with modest means to have fixed-income products as part of their portfolio. Fixed-income products should, in theory, be available for a low fee because you're not going to get a 20 percent return with fixed income. Those considerations also need to be factored in when selecting investment options for participants.

Managing Assets in a World of Higher Volatility and Lower Returns

Robert D. Arnott
Chairman, Research Affiliates, LLC
Pasadena, California
Editor, Financial Analysts Journal

The return outlook (for both stocks and bonds) is not a rosy one. Thus, investors will have to adjust their way of thinking and investing. Notably, they must realize that they cannot use just one metric of risk and that they face some significant problems when setting the policy asset mix. Furthermore, equity returns will be low, which clearly affects the risk premium. The changing U.S. demographic situation also compounds the problem for investors. Despite this dire outlook, however, several ways exist for investors to improve returns.

This presentation is not for the faint of heart. It presupposes that, going forward, equity and fixed-income returns will be lower, volatility may be higher, and market investing will be more challenging. But it is worth noting that what is on the surface a rather gloomy message is not necessarily all that gloomy. The spectrum of returns available is always wide, and in a volatile market, it is wider than ever. So, the opportunities to do well abound in this sort of environment, which is important to keep in mind when looking at aggregate returns that may be somewhat disappointing.

What Risk Matters?

One of the starting questions when managing assets is: What metrics of risk matter? A whole panoply of measures of risk have been introduced by academics, investment managers, and clients: volatility, likelihood of loss, worst-case outcomes, downside semivariance, tracking error, funding ratio shortfall, violation of account guidelines (yes, this is a risk if a manager winds up being in violation), underperforming peers, maverick risk, opportunity costs, being wrong and alone, surprise in a part of the portfolio, skewness, kurtosis, and surprise from a single failed or spectacular asset. Of these risks, I think maverick risk is the most underrated measure of risk in the investment community, particularly among academics, even though it is the risk that gets people fired more often than any other risk.

The risk that actually matters is the risk that materializes, which no one can know until after the fact. Consequently, investors need to get away from the current emphasis on trying to identify a single metric of risk and need to recognize that multiple metrics of risk matter. Take peer group risk as an example. Some investment professionals recommend ignoring peer group comparisons because they are irrelevant. From a pure investments perspective, for the most part, they are irrelevant, which would suggest moving all the way to a liability benchmark and making active bets relative to a liability-based benchmark. Others have said that they do not like losing money and advocate moving to an absolute-return framework, where they just look to produce positive returns. But if a manager does move to an absolute-return framework and does so at the wrong time and the portfolio performs badly relative to the manager's peers, the manager will be fired. So, the simple fact is that peer group comparisons matter.

The peer group comparison also matters in a more direct way. If all three sets of risk matter (i.e., if investors do not want to lose money, do not want to lag their liabilities, and do not want to underperform their peers), then managers have a vast playground in the middle, shown in **Figure 1**, within which to seek alpha and within which to seek beta-related returns in markets that are less risky relative to liabilities and less risky in absolute space than that of their peers—and yet not so far removed from their peers

Figure 1. The Tyranny of Benchmarks: Controlling the Wrong Risks

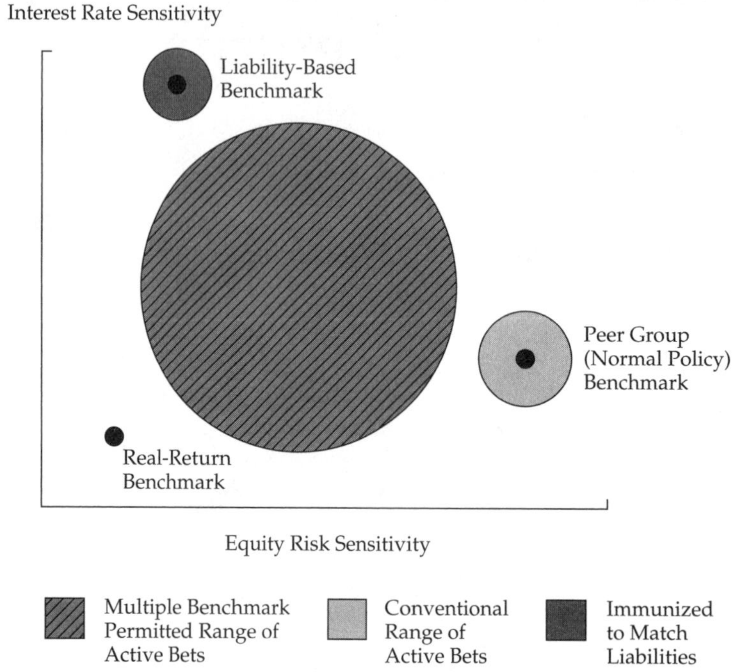

Interest Rate Sensitivity

Liability-Based Benchmark

Peer Group (Normal Policy) Benchmark

Real-Return Benchmark

Equity Risk Sensitivity

Multiple Benchmark Permitted Range of Active Bets | Conventional Range of Active Bets | Immunized to Match Liabilities

as to get them fired. I would love to see the consulting, actuarial, and accounting communities present to their clients a statement of results that shows not only fund performance and an attribution of returns—which would include such information as how it compared with the fund's peer group, as is typically done—but also how the fund performed relative to a model portfolio matching the investor's liabilities. That second step is not typically done. And even one step further, I would like the statement to show the risk the investor is taking on all three metrics.

Suppose a board of directors was presented with information for a bottom-decile year such that the company's defined-benefit (DB) plan stood to underperform its peers by 4 or 5 percent, or alternatively, lose 20 percentage points in absolute returns, or, as a third alternative, lose 30 percentage points relative to its liabilities. How many boards of directors would look at that information and be glad that they were clinging close to the peer group? Probably none. The board of directors would more than likely wonder why the plan was making such a small bet relative to peers and taking on such huge risk in absolute-return space and liability space.

This is one area where I emphatically agree with Peter Bernstein's thesis that the policy asset mix has steered investors astray.[1] The problem is not so much the use of a policy portfolio as the misuse of a policy portfolio and an obsession with a single metric of risk.

[1]See Peter L. Bernstein, "Points of Inflection: Investment Management Tomorrow," *Financial Analysts Journal* (July/August 2003):18–23.

A hypothetical portfolio will help explain this point further. Suppose you wanted to immunize your liabilities with a 15-year strip. And suppose you found a wonderful way to produce a reliable 3 percent annual alpha relative to 15-year strips. This portfolio would certainly protect you. It would defease your liabilities and lock in a return 3 percent higher than your liabilities. No board would have trouble staying the course with that sort of strategy, right? Wrong. The solid line in **Figure 2** shows the rolling three-year results of that strategy; the rolling three-year results of a 60/40 equity/fixed-income mix are shown by the dotted line. What this figure shows is that for five consecutive three-year spans, this strategy would have underperformed a 60/40 mix. How many committees would have stayed the course with that strategy even though returns were better than the 60/40 mix overall since 1990 and even though the tracking error relative to liabilities was negligible?

Reciprocally, suppose now that you are an investor with a total-return orientation and that you are a genius at selecting absolute-return managers. You wind up with a portfolio that returns 6 percent above the T-bill yield, year after year after year. Again, a dream portfolio, right? No one would ever walk away from that sort of portfolio, right? Again, wrong. The solid line in **Figure 3** is the rolling three-year performance of that strategy, and the dotted line is the rolling three-year performance of a 60/40 mix. In this case, T-bills plus 6 percent, the real-return strategy, underperformed the 60/40 mix for six consecutive three-year spans. Who has the staying power for that kind of return?

Figure 2. Fifteen-Year Strips Plus 3 Percent versus 60/40 Mix, 1990–2003

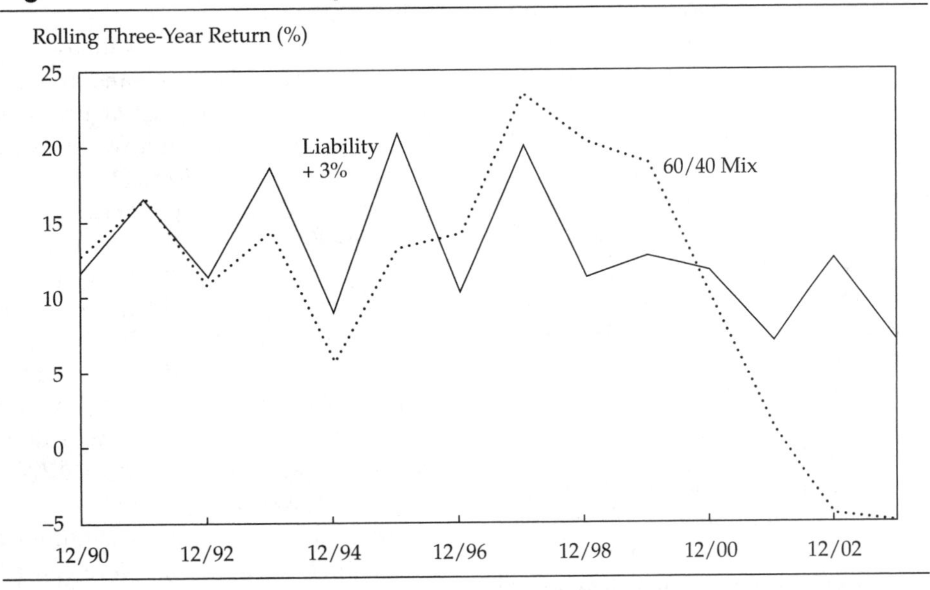

My point is that shifting the focus all the way over to an absolute-return orientation or all the way over to a liability orientation does not resolve all risk concerns. Managers have to recognize that multiple metrics of risk matter and that they cannot walk away completely from peer group comparisons if only because no one could stand the maverick risk over extended periods of time.

The Policy Portfolio Problem

Does asset allocation policy really matter? The asset allocation issue boils down to three problems: (1) asset allocation has many elements, (2) investors cannot forgo asset allocation, and (3) liabilities do not always track with assets.

Problem 1: Asset Allocation Has Many Elements. The first problem is that asset allocation has many elements. One element is the policy asset mix (i.e., what mix is likely to meet the investor's long-term needs?). Is the policy asset mix the source of some of the managers' worst errors? Absolutely. Is it misspecified? Absolutely. It is a poor fit with the needs of most funds, and importantly, it should not be static over time. It does change. The fact that it changes means that the dividing line between policy allocation and tactical asset allocation is not a clear, sharp line at all. There is a continuum.

Some people might view the policy asset mix as very slow tactical asset allocation, which (if one looks at the way most funds manage money) is a bad tactical

Figure 3. T-Bills Plus 6 Percent versus 60/40 Mix, 1990–2003

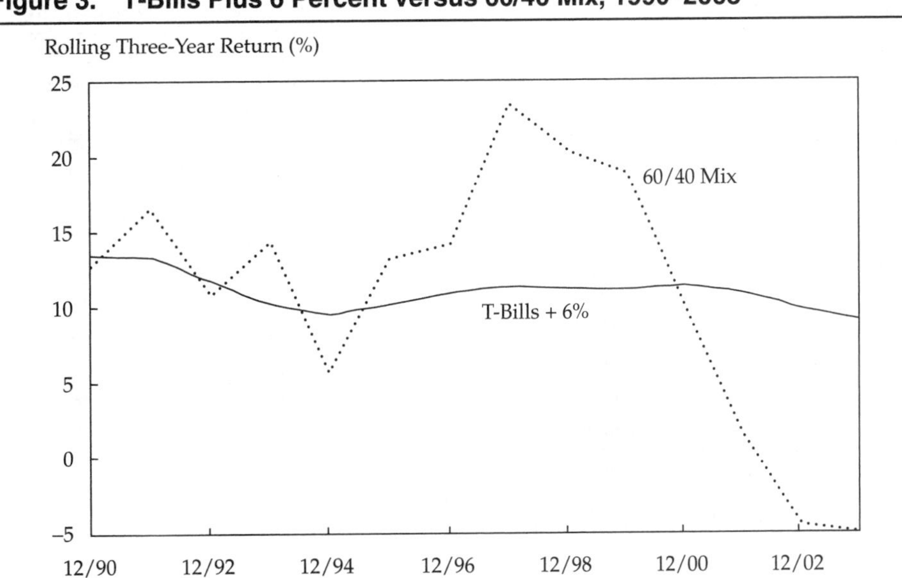

model. Allocations to equities drifted up in the 1980s and 1990s in the face of a relentless two-decade bull market. As a consequence of that effect, normal policy equity exposure was at an extreme high in 2000. Such a move has never happened before, right? Wrong. It happened in the relentless bull market leading up to 1972, before the market broke in 1973–1974.

At the other end of the spectrum is purposeful tactical asset allocation (i.e., what departures from the policy mix are likely to garner rewards?). Tactical asset allocation comes in different flavors—domestic or global, simple or sophisticated, directly moving money between markets or through overlay management. And it can be moved down a level to tactical style management within equities, for example, or up a level to embrace alternative assets in a tactical framework. These are all elements of the tactical process; they all merit careful consideration as to whether something fits with the investment program.

Interestingly, investors have shown a renewed interest in mechanistic option-replication strategies, which basically protect assets against specific risks over a specific horizon. I find it curious that long-term investors who are defeasing 20-, 30-, or 40-year liabilities are trying to protect against particular outcomes over a 1-year horizon. The popularity of costless collars, portfolio insurance, surplus insurance—whatever is used—is curious when investors are defeasing long-term obligations. But it is a real part of the world.

Problem 2: Investors Cannot Forgo Asset Allocation. The second problem is that investors cannot forgo asset allocation. Asset allocation on autopilot is a bad choice. It should be a thoughtful, well-reasoned decision.

■ *2000–03 period.* How many people remember the 2000–03 period as a fun and exciting time to be in the markets, providing great profit opportunities? Typically, not many. But it was a world with a wide spectrum of returns. **Table 1** shows that commodities were up 89 percent, emerging market debt was up 69 percent, TIPS (the common name for U.S. Treasury Inflation-Indexed Securities) were up 54 percent, and the dull, old Lehman Brothers Aggregate Bond Index was up 39 percent. Those are all good returns. In contrast, the unhedged MSCI EAFE (Europe/Australasia/Far East) Index was down 44 percent, the S&P 500 Index was down 20 percent (despite a near 30 percent return in 2003), and a 60/40 passive mix was up 4 percent.

Risk also falls along a continuum, and in the 2000–03 period, investors were concentrated in the highest risk markets, believing that these markets assured higher returns. I do not recall anything in contract law or in any documents I have signed with a broker that says the more risk I take, the more return I am assured to get. It does not work that way. Finance theory says that higher expected risk means higher expected return, but why on earth does our industry have such a problem with the concept that maybe the equity risk premium actually was negative in the year 2000? That is, maybe the long-term returns available from stocks were less than the long-term returns available from bonds when bonds were yielding 6 percent and stocks were yielding 1 percent.

Table 1. Performance by Asset Class, 2000–2003

Asset Class	Cumulative Return	Annual Standard Deviation[a]	Correlation with 60/40 Mix[a]
Commodities[b]	+89%	14%	9%
Emerging market debt	+69	12	58
TIPS composite	+54	6	–12
Long governments	+49	10	–7
Lehman Brothers Aggregate Bond Index	+39	4	1
Salomon world bonds	+38	8	–3
Ginnie Mae[c] bonds	+34	3	–5
Short-term bonds	+26	2	–17
High-yield bonds	+24	9	52
Convertible bonds	+22	15	76
60/40 passive mix	+4	11	100
S&P 500	–20	18	99
EAFE international stocks (local currency)	–44	17	73

[a]Risk and correlation from January 1997 through December 2003.
[b]Return on Dow Jones–AIG Commodity Futures Index collateralized by short-duration TIPS.
[c]Government National Mortgage Association.

The problem with 2000–2003 was not a lack of return opportunities; many markets performed very well. The problem was that one asset category (equities) performed poorly, and practically everyone was heavily concentrated in that asset class. So, it was a bear market only for those who were wedded to an equity-centric "normal portfolio."

■ *Setting reasonable return expectations.* A key element in the whole policy asset allocation debate is one of setting reasonable long-term return expectations. For bonds, the Lehman Aggregate will likely provide a long-term return of about 4 percent from current levels. After all, that is the yield! Some bond categories look better; some look worse. For stocks, a 5 percent return (on the high end) seems most likely—1.5 percent from income, 1 percent from real growth, and 2.5 percent from inflation. Although Jeremy Siegel would disagree with a 1 percent real growth number, that is what it has been for the past 75 years, for the past 100 years, and for the past 200 years give or take a half a percent.[2] Why has this number been so low when GDP growth has been 2.5–3 percent? I will come back to that point later, but earnings and dividend growth are structurally lower than, indeed must be lower than, GDP growth.

The implication is that balanced portfolios will likely deliver up to about 5 percent minus fees and trading, and the situation can be viewed in one of two ways. One way is to say: "I was counting on 9 percent. I need 9 percent." The other way is to say: "If 5 percent is what the markets are going to deliver, I need to work that figure into my planning. I need to count on a reasonable expectation, although I can certainly seek more." Expecting more does not make it happen. Wishful thinking is not a strategy. There is no harm in seeking more, but there is harm in expecting more or counting on more. Expecting 9 percent because that is the number used as the pension return assumption in calculating corporate earnings does not make it happen. If it did, why not assume 20 percent, or, what the heck, assume 100 percent a year?

Equity returns are likely to match bond returns in the next 25 years, which implies about a 5 percent annual return for stocks, bonds, and balanced funds. That is the upside if there is no reversion to the mean. I would disagree with those who say that 2003 disproves the low equity risk premium. It does not. I am describing an equity risk premium based on long-term return expectations. One can be bullish in a secular bear market. One can believe that markets on a tactical, short-term basis are headed up. A big difference exists, however, between short-term returns and long-term internal rates of return. I am focused on the long-term internal rates of return, which do not look pretty.

[2]See Jeremy Siegel's presentation in this proceedings.

There is no way out for the investment community at large, although certainly some funds will do better than others. That is, the opportunities to find interesting investment returns in other markets are liquid enough that the largest fund sponsors in the world could easily do it, but the 5 or 10 largest fund sponsors in the world could not do it at the same time and all get good results.

The opportunities are simple. An investor can make about a half a percent from systematic rebalancing, about a percent from alpha in asset selection if the investor is good at choosing active managers, about a percent from successful tactical asset allocation if the investor can identify managers or individuals with skill in tactical asset allocation, and about a percent with material allocations to selected opportunistic alternative markets. By doing all that, the best practices funds may actually achieve their actuarial rate of return, but the majority of the marketplace will not.

Problem 3: Liabilities Do Not Always Track with Assets. The third problem is that liabilities do not always track with assets. I will delve deeper into this problem later in this presentation when I discuss the role of DB and defined-contribution (DC) plans.

Low Equity Returns

I believe that the current bull market is the eye of the storm for equities; it is not the end of the storm. I see several risks that are likely to depress long-term internal rates of return for equities in the years ahead, and one of these is immediate: Earnings quality is far lower than most investors believe. Another one is that valuation is still high by historical standards.

Quality of Earnings. The year 2000 was an economic peak, a market peak, and an earnings peak. S&P 500 reported earnings were $54 a share. Wall Street, however, was saying "never mind the $54 a share; operating earnings are $68 a share." So, what are operating earnings? Operating earnings are earnings after stripping away everything that went wrong. Suppose an investor wants to perform fundamental analysis on AOL Time Warner with its $54 billion write-off. Does the investor include the $54 billion loss in calculating the company's P/E? Of course not. Using operating earnings to value a company with truly extraordinary write-offs makes sense. But what is extraordinary for a company is not extraordinary for the market at large. Write-offs are a normal part of the economy. So, using operating earnings for the economy is at best naive and at worst a fraud.

But back to the S&P 500 earnings at $54 a share in 2000 when the market was at 30 times earnings. How real was the $54 a share? Companies were assuming a 9.5 percent return on their pension assets. Bonds were yielding 6 percent; stocks were barely yielding 1 percent. Investors would have had to assume astronomical growth on equity portfolios to get a 9.5 percent total return from a balanced portfolio at the time. If companies had merely assumed a 6 percent return on their pension assets, they could have locked in risk-free government bonds and been assured of defeasing their liabilities. Aggregate earnings, however, would have been $8 lower. I would argue that the $8 savings on pension expense was wishful thinking on the companies' part, not reality. Continuing on, if management stock options were expensed, earnings would have been $6 lower. And because of fiscal-year 2000 earnings restatements by the likes of Enron Corporation, Global Crossing, and MCI, $3 of earnings has already evaporated. The end result is that investors are looking at S&P 500 earnings of about $37 a share ($54 less $8 less $6 less $3) at a market peak, at an economic peak, and at a cyclical earnings peak. If that was our latest peak earnings, what are the normalized earnings? They are more than likely lower, at $30–$35. Assuming current normalized earnings are in that ballpark, this would put the market at north of 30 times earnings again.

Valuation Levels. Figure 4 shows the market P/E using a variant on Shiller's P/E calculation. Shiller likes to use 10-year smoothed nominal earnings. I like to use 10-year smoothed real earnings and divide that figure into the real S&P 500 price to make things more directly comparable between high- and low-inflation eras. This figure, which goes back 130 years, shows several things quite vividly.

First, the recent equity bubble was extraordinary. It was beyond anything seen before, and more than that, it was beyond anything that people could have imagined possible before it happened.

Second, the wiggles on the chart are classic bull and bear markets and are subsumed within major secular bull and bear markets. Those secular bull and bear markets span decades, not years. The general consensus in the marketplace is that bull and bear markets are reasonably normal and that investors should expect a bear market every now and again. What is not widely recognized is the risk of a secular bear market after a bubble or after a secular bull market peak. In the past, secular peaks occurred in 1901, 1929, and 1965; these peaks were followed by 17- to 20-year secular bear markets spanning three to five bull and bear market cycles.

After the largest bubble in U.S. capital market history, should investors reasonably expect a secular bear market that is milder or shorter than past ones? I do not think so.

Third and last, secular bear markets do not end when the market returns to historical normal valuation levels. They end when markets are cheap.

The Equity Risk Premium

Peter Bernstein and I wrote a paper entitled "What Risk Premium Is 'Normal'?"[3] It is a paper that I am very proud to have been a part of. We examined the issue of the risk premium from a number of perspectives.

[3] Robert D. Arnott and Peter L. Bernstein, "What Risk Premium Is 'Normal'?" *Financial Analysts Journal* (March/April 2002):64–85.

Figure 4. P/E Based on Smoothed 10-Year Real Earnings, 1871–March 2004

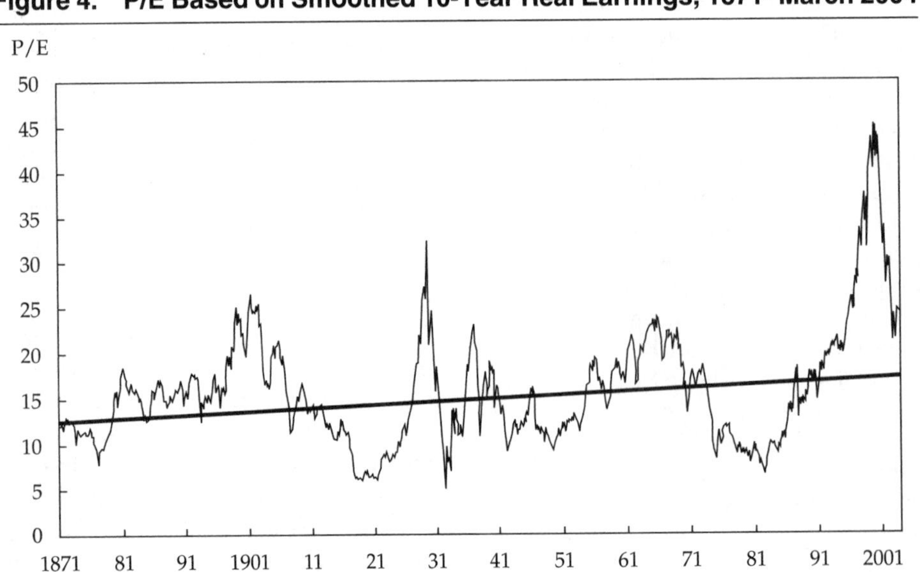

Any investment has three components of return: income, growth in income, and multiple expansion. The returns in the Ibbotson data that form the bible for the investment industry show a roughly 7 percent real return for stocks over the past 78 years. Going back further, one finds a 6.5–7 percent real return over the past 200 years. **Table 2** shows the return attribution going back to 1926; 4.3 percent was from income, 1.1 percent was from growth, and 1.5 percent was from change in valuation levels—multiple expansion, failing dividend yields, rising P/Es, and so on. Do investors dare extrapolate those return figures from today's valuation levels? I think doing so would be dangerous. A lot of the forecasting of returns in the investment industry comes from graduates of the institute for advanced hindsight, research into what should have been.

Table 2. Real-Return Attribution, January 1926–March 2004

Measure	77 Years, Starting 1926	Prospects from April 2004
Average dividend yield	4.3%	1.5%
Growth in real dividends	1.1	1.1
Change in valuation levels[a]	1.5	?
Cumulative real return	6.9	±2.6
Less average real bond yield	3.3	2.3[b]
Less bond valuation change[c]	−0.9	?
Cumulative risk premium	4.7%	±0.3%

[a]Yields went from 5.4 percent to 1.5 percent, representing a 1.5 percent annual increase in the price/dividend valuation level.

[b]Yield on U.S. government inflation-indexed bonds.

[c]Bond yields fell during this period, and real yields on reinvestment were also poor during much of this span.

Source: Based on data from Ibbotson Associates.

What is the implication for the long-term forward risk premium? Currently, the dividend yield is 1.5 percent. Historical, normal real earnings and dividend growth have been just over 1 percent. P/E expansion can hardly be expected. So, as shown in Table 2, just over 2.5 percent is a reasonable expectation for real returns on stocks. And this figure does not take account of any reversion to the mean. It assumes that P/Es and dividend yields stay right where they are. Others can quibble with that number by playing around with growth rates and the dividend yield and by saying stock buybacks are a hidden form of dividends. But it is hard to stretch that figure more than about a half a percent. Finally, investors can get 2.3 percent from long TIPS, which are backed by the full faith and credit of the U.S. government. Subtracting the long TIPS yield gives a 0.3 percent risk premium, which is worrisome.

This risk premium can similarly be arrived at by beginning with the same 1.5 percent dividend yield, adding 2.7 percent for the long-term real GDP growth, and subtracting 1.6 percent for growth from new enterprise creation. The result is a long-term real return from stocks of 2.6 percent and thus a risk premium of 0.3 percent after subtracting the current 2.3 percent long TIPS yield.

Suppose that 200 years ago someone in your family put $100 in the stock market and said that the investment would be released to future descendents in 200 years. Today, that $100 would be worth half a billion dollars. In real terms, however, the investment is reduced to about $25 million, which is still good. Now, suppose your ancestors changed the deal in one seemingly minor regard. Suppose your ancestors said: "Bonds are for income, and stocks are for growth. I am going to take the income out of this portfolio, spend the dividends, and leave 100 percent of the growth to my descendents." That $100 grows, in real terms, to $1,500 in 200 years. All of a sudden, this investment is not so impressive.

What about growth? **Figure 5** shows how well dividends and earnings track economic growth. The solid heavy line shows growth in the U.S. economy. Many believe earnings, dividends, and share prices should grow with the economy in the long run. This notion is not true for a simple reason. Economic growth has two primary engines: the growth of existing enterprises and the creation of new enterprises, entrepreneurial capitalism. Existing stock market investments allow investors to participate in the growth of existing enterprises but miss the boat on the majority of economic growth that is caused by new enterprise creation resulting from entrepreneurial capitalism. Because more than half of real GDP growth comes from entrepreneurial capitalism, real earnings and dividends should collectively grow a bit below half the rate of economic growth. The solid thin line in Figure 5 shows the growth in real per capita GDP, which is itself an impressive story. It has had 25-fold growth in 200 years.

The dotted line shows stock prices, and the dashed line shows dividends. Finally, the light gray line shows earnings. Are aggregate earnings growing with the overall economy? No. They are growing in line with real per capita GDP, which is a proxy for productivity growth. Productivity growth flows roughly equally to workers in the form of rising wages and to investors in the form of rising earnings and dividends. So, those who suggest that earnings and dividend growth can exceed GDP growth are postulating a future so radically different from the past as to be implausible.

Figure 5. Growth of Dividends, Earnings, and the Economy, 1800–2003

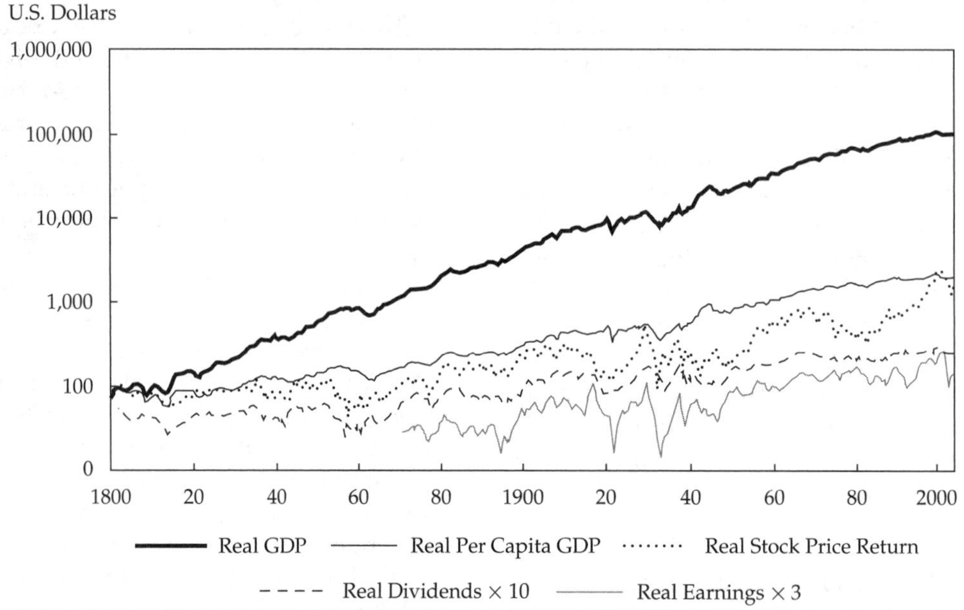

U.S. Dollars

1,000,000
100,000
10,000
1,000
100
0

1800 20 40 60 80 1900 20 40 60 80 2000

Real GDP — Real Per Capita GDP — Real Stock Price Return — Real Dividends × 10 — Real Earnings × 3

Source: Based on data from First Quadrant.

It is also useful to disaggregate those returns historically. The returns over the past 200 years were wonderful, but that is the past. It is a past consisting of average yields of 5 percent. The present and the future consist of yields lower than that unless markets revalue to a materially lower level. **Figure 6** shows the results of disaggregating returns on the various return components. Dividends are the overwhelmingly dominant factor. They are easily more than 80 percent of the real return from stocks in the long run. Valuation expansion, in contrast, was flat for 180 years with a lot of wiggles along the way and then soared from 1982 to 2000. Real dividend growth, driven by underlying economic growth, was rock steady, rising fivefold in 200 years. Inflation, the second biggest component of the return, was bigger than real dividend growth, which is a surprise.

What about payout ratios? Roger Ibbotson and others have argued that because payout ratios are lower than ever before, retained earnings can sustain growth faster than ever before. Remember that those retained earnings were plowed into dreadful investments in telecom, Internet infrastructure, and other not-so-fabulous investments in the future growth of corporate earnings. Retained earnings tend to be a basis for corporate empire building. **Figure 7** is a graph of the post–World War II period comparing the payout ratio at the start of the period with subsequent 10-year earnings growth. This figure shows that when payout ratios have historically been high, real earnings growth has been extremely high. When payout ratios have been low, real earnings growth has been anemic; in fact, it has often been negative. Such a strong positive relationship is startling in something that finance theory suggests should have a powerful negative relationship. All MBA students have been taught that companies can retain more earnings to invest for faster growth. The implication of these data is that beyond a certain threshold, and it is not a large threshold, retaining more earnings is not beneficial because the retained earnings wind up being plowed into frivolous enterprises that lose money and restrain company growth.[4]

Back to the risk premium itself. How important is the risk premium? Suppose that the belief that stocks normally beat bonds by 5 percent a year is true and that investors can bank on that return. So, in the very long run with normal volatility, stocks will beat bonds by 5 percent a year, which compounds mightily. After 10 years, an investor will have an average of 70 percent more wealth with stocks than with bonds, but there is a risk. With 15 percent volatility between stocks and bonds, the investor would have an 85 percent chance of more wealth with stocks and a 15 percent chance of less wealth. After 20 years, the investor would have 170 percent more wealth with stocks with 95 percent odds of success. Stocks for the long run? You bet. This line of reasoning is the basis for much of the cult of equities that dominates the thinking in the investment world.

[4]See Robert D. Arnott and Clifford S. Asness, "Surprise! Higher Dividends = Higher Earnings Growth," *Financial Analysts Journal* (January/February 2003):70–87.

Figure 6. Growth of $100 Invested in U.S. Equities, 1800–2002

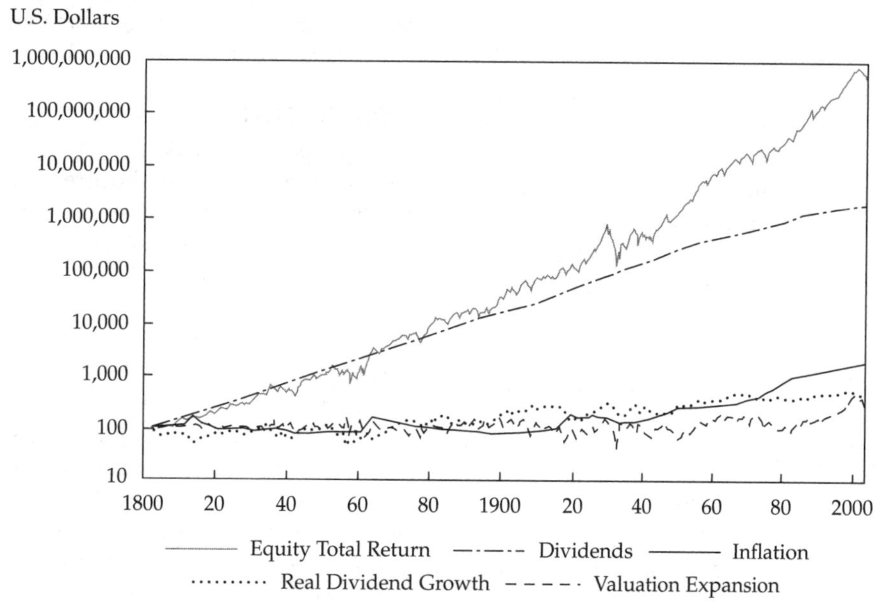

U.S. Dollars
1,000,000,000
100,000,000
10,000,000
1,000,000
100,000
10,000
1,000
100
10
1800
20
40
60
80
1900
20
40
60
80
2000
Equity Total Return
Dividends
Inflation
Real Dividend Growth
Valuation Expansion

Sources: Based on data from G. William Schwert, "Indexes of United States Stock Prices from 1802 to 1987," *Journal of Business* (July 1990):399–426 for 1801–1870, a blend of data from G. William Schwert and Jeremy J. Siegel, *Stocks for the Long Run*, 3rd ed. (New York: McGraw-Hill, 2002) for 1871–1925, and S&P 500 data since 1926.

Figure 7. Payout Ratio and Subsequent 10-Year Earnings Growth, 1946–1991

Next 10-Year Earnings Growth Rate (%)
12
10
8
6
4
2
0
–2
–4
35
45
55
65
75
85
95
Payout Ratio (%)

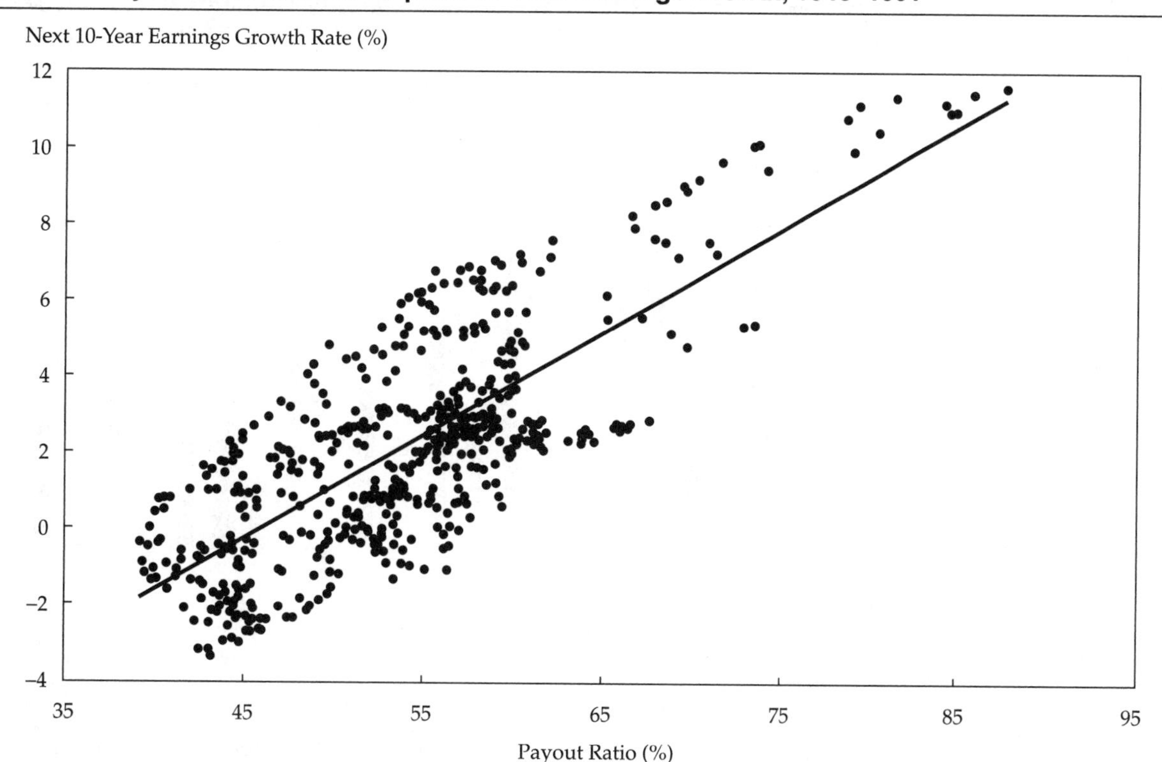

Source: Based on data from First Quadrant.

Now, suppose the risk premium is only 2 percent a year with the same level of risk.[5] If the risk premium is only 2 percent a year, do investors have to wait 50 years to get that 95 percent chance of success? No, they have to wait about 200 years! Even at a 2 percent excess return of stocks relative to bonds, many investors would stay with an equity-biased portfolio. The notion that a 5 percent risk premium is needed to justify a 60/40 or 70/30 equity/bond portfolio mix is not correct. But to have 95 percent confidence that that mix is the right choice, investors have to wait a long, long, long time. In light of that analysis, think about what would happen if the risk premium is zero: Investors would have 50/50 odds of stocks beating bonds . . . forever.

The Bond Picture

So, what about bonds? Much of this discussion probably sounds like equity bashing, but bonds are not a whole lot better off. **Figure 8** is a graph of the past 30 years. The bars represent total bond performance per year, and the line shows the yield. Bonds returned more than their yield in 15 of the last 23 years. This is possible with a fixed-income asset because investors receive capital gains whenever yields fall in addition to the coupon yield. But bond capital gains are a lot easier to get if the starting point yield is 14 percent rather than 4 percent. Therein lies the problem.

Demographics: The Big Risk Factor

Demographics is the 800-pound gorilla that everyone seems to be ignoring. Future trends require that returns be lower than they are now. **Figure 9** shows life expectancy over the last 60 years and over the next 45 years. Notice that when Social Security benefits first became payable in 1940, life expectancy was 63 years—for men it was 61 years, and men were the dominant part of the workforce back then. So, in 1940, the U.S. government was telling its citizens that if they lived to age 65, it would take care of them. It is not an expensive program if most people are dead four years before they are eligible to receive benefits. It is a lot more expensive, however, if the average person is living 12 years past the retirement age and those who make it to the retirement age are living an average of 18 years longer. The notion that the retirement age should not move with longevity is, I think, a quaint fiction.

One aspect of this puzzle that has been studied a great deal is the notion of dependency ratio: the number of retirees per working-age person if one assumes

[5] I am indebted to André Perold for the idea for this analysis.

Figure 8. Lehman Treasury Index Returns and 10-Year Constant Maturity Treasury Yields, 1973–2002

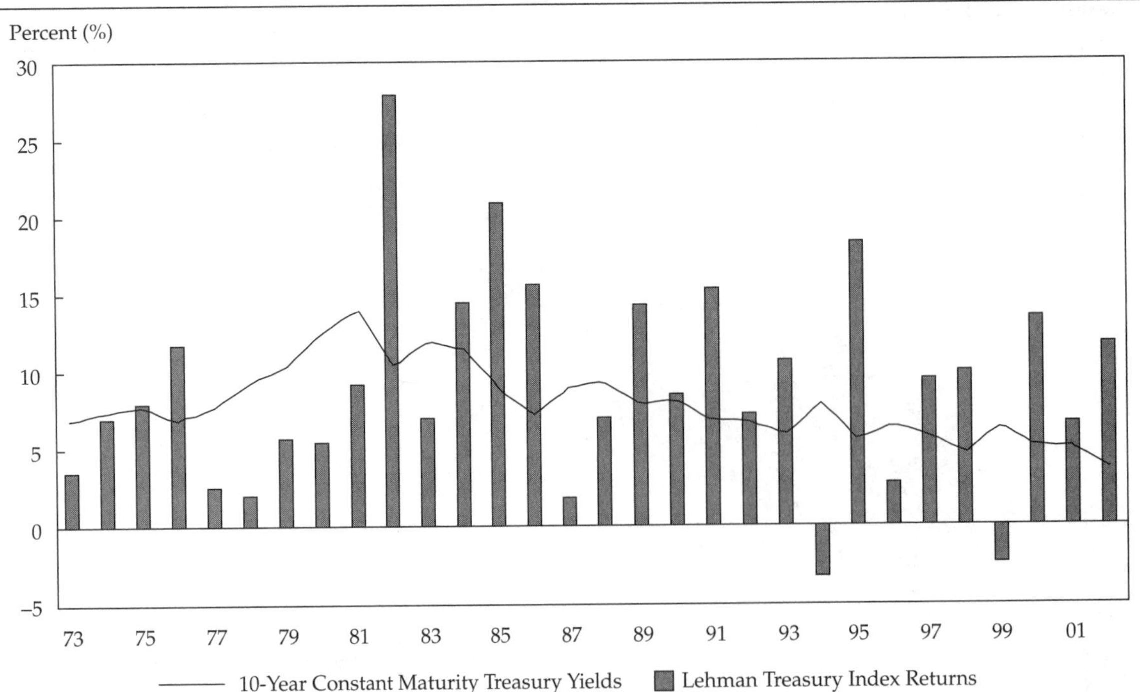

Note: The Lehman Treasury Index is an unmanaged index consisting of public obligations of the U.S. Treasury with a remaining maturity of one year or more.

Sources: Based on data from Bloomberg Financial Markets and PIMCO (Pacific Investment Management Company).

Figure 9. U.S. Life Expectancy, 1940–2050

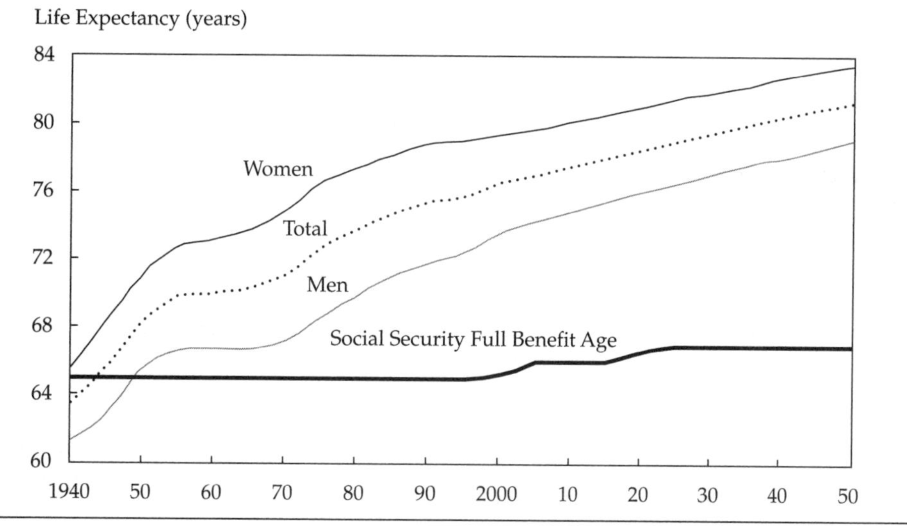

Source: Based on data from First Quadrant.

retirees are all older than age 65 and people aged 20–65 years are all eligible for the workforce. As can be seen in **Figure 10**, the dependency ratio rose quickly in the 1950s and 1960s and then remained steady for 40 years. It is now poised to take off, starting an inexorable climb as Baby Boomers begin to retire around 2010.

Anne Casscells and I took this analysis and reversed it.[6] We looked at the implications of maintaining current support ratios. What we found was that the normal retirement age would have to rise for the Baby Boomers to age 72. Admittedly, some would retire early at age 65, and some would retire late, working until age 80 and in some cases well past 80, but age 72 would be the norm if support ratios cannot rise. I would argue that support ratios can rise a little bit; immigration can help some with the support ratios. But the simple fact is that with longer life spans, people will have to work longer, and it is naive to suppose otherwise.

Consider now what the demographic situation means for the markets. The first column of **Table 3** shows the correlation of various assets relative to a 60/40 mix. And the next columns show the tracking error of each market, measured relative to T-bills, long bonds, and TIPS. The final column is the average

[6]Robert D. Arnott and Anne Casscells, "Demographics and Capital Market Returns," *Financial Analysts Journal* (March/April 2003):20–29.

Figure 10. Dependency Ratio, 1950–2050

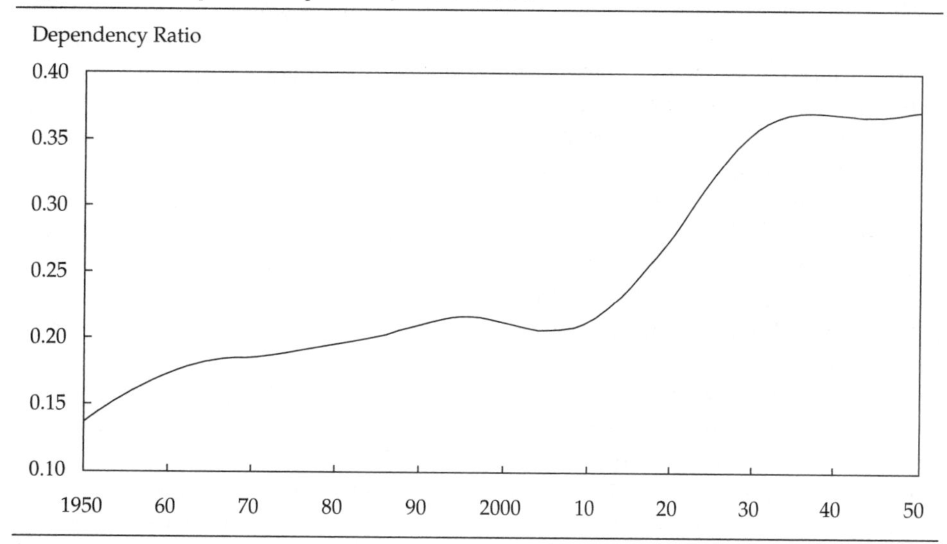

Source: Based on data from First Quadrant.

Table 3. Correlation and Risk by Asset Class, 1997–2003

Asset Class	Correlation with 60/40 Mix	Risk[a] vs. T-Bills	Risk[a] vs. Long Bonds	Risk[a] vs. TIPS	Combined Risk[b] (average)
Commodities[b]	5%	13%	14%	12%	13 (med)
Long governments	–12	8	0	6	3 (low)
TIPS composite	–23	4	6	0	1 (low)
Lehman Brothers Aggregate Bond Index	–2	4	5	3	4 (low)
Emerging market debt	+57	19	21	19	25 (high)
Ginnie Mae bonds	–6	2	7	3	3 (low)
Short-term bonds	–18	2	7	4	3 (low)
Salomon world bonds	–8	6	7	6	6 (low)
High-yield bonds	51	7	11	8	14 (med)
60/40 passive mix[c]	100	10	13	11	21 (high)
Convertible bonds	76	13	17	14	22 (high)
S&P 500[c]	98	16	19	17	27 (high)
EAFE international stocks	82	17	21	18	27 (high)

[a]Risks are calculated over past 75 months from February 1997 to April 2003.
[b]Return on Dow Jones–AIG Commodity Futures Index collateralized by short-duration TIPS.
[c]Average of three risk measures is adjusted up or down by correlation divided by 10.

across all of these risks (i.e., a composite score of risk). The result is an array of low-risk assets, an array of high-risk assets, and a few assets stuck in the middle. Where does the institutional community largely position its portfolios? The S&P 500, MSCI EAFE, and 60/40 passive mix. Compared with those assets, many lower-risk assets have produced higher returns in the 1997–2003 period, thus confounding those who assume that higher risk is assured higher return.

Demographics matters because as Baby Boomers age, they are going to be looking to reduce their risk exposure in U.S. stocks, emerging market stocks and bonds, MSCI EAFE stocks, and convertibles either through proxies in the pension world or through direct personal decisions. Those are the asset categories that are the highest risk and that represent the greatest threat to retirement security.

The assets they will sell last depend on investor objectives. That is, the ones that would be the best fit with their long-term needs differ depending on goals. For those wanting to avoid losses, Ginnie Mae, cash, short-term bonds, TIPS, and the Lehman Aggregate represent assets that they would likely sell last to protect their livelihood and to spend later in retirement. For those desiring income preservation, long governments, TIPS, and the Lehman Aggregate would be sold last. For those wanting to preserve the real spending power of their portfolio, long TIPS, TIPS, and commodities would be sold last. Notice that mainstream bonds have dropped out of the picture and have been replaced with commodities. The implications of demographics are rather straightforward and have a bearing on capital markets.

Ways to Improve Returns

The outlook may not be bright, but investors have three (and a half) ways to improve returns.

The first approach is to expand asset class selection. If stocks and bonds are not sufficient, look elsewhere. A whole spectrum of asset class opportunities exist. Some of them are interesting most all the time, and some are interesting one year and not the next.

The second way is to seek alpha. That is, try to identify managers who can outperform stocks, outperform bonds, outperform in emerging market debt, outperform in commodities, and so on. Or if the investor has no skill in identifying those superior managers in advance, at least shut off the pain by avoiding negative alpha.

The third way to improve returns is to actively manage the asset mix. That is, move out of markets that are popular, trendy, and accordingly priced to provide lower future returns and move into markets that are attractively priced (often because they are out of favor and uncomfortable for investors to invest in).

And finally (what I call the "half") is to use leverage. Certainly, investors can take all three paths in parallel. And those who are really adventuresome can choose all "four" approaches by leveraging the other three.

Stacking multiple sources of profit is an interesting way to deal with lower returns and higher volatility in the markets. That is, make opportunistic use of alternative assets when stocks and bonds are unattractive, which I would argue is not an inaccurate characterization of today's market opportunities. Next, add in successful fund managers within their own asset classes, and finally, add value added from an active asset allocation process. The result is alpha stacking. Suppose an investor gets a 2–3 percent real return from mainstream stocks and bonds. If each of those three sources of alpha is only 1 percent, adding them together gives a 300 bp improvement in returns, which gives the investor a 5–6 percent real-return opportunity.

The point is not to just roll over and say "oh gosh, returns are going to be awful" and hope that the pain goes away. The correct response is to do something about it.

The Role of DC Plans

More money is now invested in DC plans than in DB plans. This trend is adding to the problems that I have been discussing in this presentation.

Suppose a 30-year-old employee is making $35,000 a year. The company tells this employee that it has a great 401(k) plan and that if her income grows 4 percent a year, if she makes 8 percent on her assets, and if she sets aside 6 percent, which is matched with 3 percent from the company, her final salary will be $138,000 at age 65 and the assets in her 401(k) will be almost $1 million. At an 8 percent rate, she could buy an annuity that would pay her $88,000 a year until age 85, which is close to two-thirds of her final pay. Social Security is added on top of that $88,000, so she will be just fine in retirement. That is the message employees are getting, and 8 percent is not an uncommon return assumption that employers are encouraging employees to consider.

In acknowledging that this is no longer a world of high returns, a focus on real inflation-adjusted terms becomes critical. Suppose now that this employee's real wage growth is only 2 percent and her real asset returns are only 3 percent, although I would argue that 3 percent is a stretch for most investors. Her final salary will have doubled to $70,000 in real spendable terms by the time she reaches age 65, and her real assets will be about a quarter million instead of 1 million—a big step down. If she wants to retire on two-thirds of her pay, she had better work until age 74, not 65.

What happens for an employee who starts 10 years later at age 40 and who is making $45,000 a year? With the same assumptions as in the previous example (2 percent real wage growth and 3 percent real asset growth), this employee's final real salary will again be roughly $70,000, but real assets will not even be $200,000. A lot of people look at $200,000 in a 401(k) account and think it is a lot of money. But it does not last long. If this employee buys a real indexed annuity at a 3 percent real rate, he will have $12,000 a year to retire on. He will have to retire at age 76 to get two-thirds of his final salary.

Finally, some employees who are 50 years old are just starting to think about retirement. If such an employee has a current salary of $55,000 and again has real income growth of 2 percent and real asset growth of 3 percent, he will have a final real salary of just more than $70,000 and his 401(k) will have $114,000 in it. At age 65, he will be retiring on $7,000 a year. To retire on two-thirds of his final pay, he will have to work until age 79.

Conclusion

The concrete implications of lower returns are straightforward, and the existence of DC plans does not change the reality. The simple fact is that with people living longer, people will have to work longer. DC plans hide the problem for a while because, unfortunately, employees do not understand the pricing of the liability associated with their prospective retirement. The losses they saw in their 401(k) statements from 2000–2002 were not half the problem. The larger portion of the problem was that the cost of funding a retirement annuity went up by more than their assets went down. If their assets were down 25 percent, the cost of funding a retirement went up 35–40 percent. So, in terms of purchasing power for retirement, they lost almost half their money in those three years . . . and do not even know it.

The time they will come to realize it is when they start to think about actually cutting the rope and retiring. They will be looking at their 401(k) and realizing that they cannot afford to retire yet. They are going to be working for years after their intended retirement time, and they are not going to be happy about it.

I would argue that the big story in the pension world in the coming quarter century will be how we break the pension promise to the Baby Boomer generation, not whether we do so.

Question and Answer Session

Robert D. Arnott

Question: How do you get 0.5 percent from simply rebalancing?

Arnott: There is lots of evidence of modest mean reversion, although it acts slowly over time. For instance, if you take rolling 10-year returns for stocks, there is a correlation of almost *minus* 40 percent between last decade's return and the subsequent decade's return. Thus, mean reversion is strong when you're looking at long spans. If you get mean reversion, it does imply profitability from rebalancing.

If you look at the historical data in alpha terms, rebalancing is worth about a half a percent. I say "in alpha terms" because if you were rebalancing in the 1990s, you were constantly selling equities and buying bonds and licking your wounds a year later for having done so. That rebalancing in the 1990s produced alpha but not incremental return. It produced alpha by lowering your risk even more than it cost you in return.

Today, if stocks and bonds are priced to offer similar returns, all of a sudden alpha and incremental returns are pretty much one and the same thing. So, that's where you get the extra half percent.

Question: Given your risk premium, why wouldn't hedge funds be an attractive investment if they earn 3 percent after fees?

Arnott: I'm invested in hedge funds, although not a lot. I think that carefully selected hedge funds can be a good investment for a taxable investor. But I also think expectations for hedge funds need to be a lot lower than they are. People buy hedge funds expecting double-digit returns, which is not going to happen for the most part. Furthermore, I think the notion of buying low-risk hedge funds makes no sense for the taxable investor. For the taxable investor, if you're going into the hedge fund world, go for the very-high-risk hedge funds and just put less money in them.

Question: With floating-rate investments, why wouldn't active bond investing be an attractive way to go? Are you giving bonds enough credit?

Arnott: The marketplace is currently pricing bonds at a 4 percent yield, overall. I think any asset class is interesting if it is priced to offer an attractive forward-looking rate of return. I think mainstream investment-grade bonds are a little worrisome. There are mounting inflation pressures, but those are also already partly priced into long bonds. Inflation could rise to 3–4 percent, and a long bond yielding 5 percent is still OK. I think the threat of inflation to bonds is a little overstated, but it is still a threat.

Inflation is not a threat, however, to certain categories. Emerging market debt gives a nice enough premium yield to absorb material rates of inflation. TIPS explicitly protect you from inflation. There are lots of interesting categories in the bond market, and in fact, broadly stated, my own investments are heavily tilted toward bonds, but I have zero in mainstream investment-grade U.S. debt.

Question: What is the liability benchmark when the benefits are indexed?

Arnott: If the benefits are indexed, it is the same sort of situation as a university endowment or a foundation. You have anticipated spending that you want to sustain in real terms, in inflation-indexed terms. The risk-minimizing portfolio for that is a laddered portfolio of long TIPS with a distribution stream matching the real payouts. But the yield doesn't come anywhere near the 5 percent spending that most endowments or foundations are funding.

Question: Could you address Jeremy Siegel's point that lower payouts lead to higher earnings growth?

Arnott: Jeremy Siegel's findings were diametrically opposite to mine. His method of analysis was to look at long secular regimes, and I would say that he was correct. Although based on three statistically independent samples, there's not much to go on.

Question: Are Asian investors, the Chinese in particular, coming in just in time to offset the demographic demise in the United States of supply and demand for stocks?

Arnott: Right now Asian investors are buying our assets at a prodigious pace. What this thesis suggests is that they're going to buy them at a more prodigious pace in the future, sufficient to compensate for all Baby Boomers trying to sell assets to fund purchases of goods and services in their retirement. I think that's a stretch. For the most powerful economy in the world to be looking to the Third World to bail it out by selling us inexpensive goods in exchange for I-O-Us is a dangerous hypothesis.

The Long-Run Equity Risk Premium

Jeremy J. Siegel
Russell E. Palmer Professor of Finance
The Wharton School of the University of Pennsylvania
Philadelphia

Peter Bernstein's "points of inflection" raise some important issues about research, indexing, benchmarking, and the "long-only" constraint. Underlying these inflection points is the question of how the equity market will perform in the future. Historically, the equity market has returned almost 7 percent a year after inflation, but based on various assumptions, the future return looks to be more in the 5–6 percent range. Nonetheless, equities should still offer a reasonable risk premium over bonds.

This presentation is composed of two parts. The first part contains my comments on Peter Bernstein's "points of inflection": research, indexing, benchmarking, and the "long-only" constraint. The second part addresses my view of future stock and bond returns. As part of this discussion, I will analyze the current valuation of the market and delve into what I see as the forward-looking equity risk premium.

Bernstein's Points of Inflection

Peter Bernstein has identified four points of inflection in the investment management industry: research, indexing, benchmarking, and the long-only constraint.[1] By points of inflection, he means fundamental shifts in the way the investment profession looks at these issues.

Benchmarking and the Long-Only Constraint. First, let me note the two points where I think Peter is right on: equity benchmarks and long-only constraints.

■ *Benchmarking.* I have always thought that the small stock/large stock and value stock/growth stock dichotomies were rather artificial. I am quite aware that they have long been identified as factors in the Fama–French multifactor models of security returns. Nevertheless, they are not necessarily natural dichotomies where investors or analysts have expertise. Historically, an analyst or portfolio manager became a specialist in a particular industry or group of industries. Indeed, the increased stress on industry sector weightings in recent years indicates that the study of industry prospects is a very important factor in investment analysis.

Value/growth and large/small dichotomies do not naturally break down into industries. I believe that investment professionals should invest wherever they find "value." I much prefer to go to one professional money manager that can buy any stock rather than to four managers that specialize in each of the four value/growth and large/small sectors and then find someone else to tell me how to weight them. The lack of money managers that put all these parts together represents, in my opinion, an abdication of responsibility on the part of the investment profession.

■ *Long-only.* On the long-only issue, I wholeheartedly agree that managers should have far fewer restrictions on putting short positions in their portfolios. Many long-only portfolios can be converted into long–short portfolios by taking a short position in the S&P 500 Index or an appropriate benchmark index.

But frequently, a manager will want to have a greater negative weight on a stock than its share in the market, which requires active shorting of the shares. Thus, I agree that the short restriction should be removed.

Research. On the research issue, a conflict of interest has always existed between analysts doing objective research on companies and their firms' investment banking arms that are trying to woo (or

[1]See Peter L. Bernstein, "Points of Inflection: Investment Management Tomorrow," *Financial Analysts Journal* (July/August 2003):18–23.

maintain) the same companies as clients. Has it gotten worse? Yes, perhaps, but it is always worse during bubbles, and we just passed through the biggest bubble in history.

I have noted that despite these conflicts and the market bubble, brokerage recommendations still move markets. And a good bit of academic research actually supports that those recommendations, even risk adjusted, at least match and may even beat the market.[2] So, for all the sins of the brokerage houses, I am not sure we are going to see substantial changes.

One change to be noted, however, is that individual investors have seen a substantial shift from transaction-based brokerage costs to asset-based wrap fees. This shift has occurred more rapidly than I expected, and it does change incentives in the right direction. Whether money managers are worth their fees is another hotly debated issue.

Indexing. The most contentious point Peter has raised is about indexing. Peter has suggested that the dominance of large stocks, the ability to game the index, and the inability to match the entire market has damaged indexing. But I disagree with Peter on those points.

Peter claimed that the largest stocks have become a bigger proportion of the overall market value. But that is not the case. Research that I have done using CRSP databases, indicated in **Figure 1**, shows that the market capitalization of the largest 20 stocks as a percentage of the total market value of the S&P 500 has declined, not increased, over time. The same result holds for the top 50 stocks and the top 100 stocks. It is just not true that the biggest stocks occupy a larger share of the market value today than they did in earlier years.

Peter also mentioned that many of the smaller issues within the Wilshire 5000 Index make it a difficult pool in which to fully invest. But one mutual fund company is doing a good job of just that. The Vanguard Total Stock Market Fund, which has been around since April 1992, is designed to mimic the Wilshire Total Market Index, and over the past 11 years, it has trailed the Wilshire by only 19 bps a year. The greatest amount by which the annual return on the fund exceeded the Wilshire Index was 32 bps, and its maximum shortfall was 66 bps. But in recent years, its deviations have become much smaller. Although the fund does not own all the 6,500 or so stocks now in the index, it clearly does an excellent job of tracking the market.

[2]See Michael Mikhail, Paul Asquith, and Andrea Au, "Information Content of Equity Analyst Reports," *Journal of Financial Economics* (forthcoming), and Brad Barber, Reuven Lehavy, Maureen McNichols, and Brett Trueman, "Reassessing the Returns to Analysts' Stock Recommendations," *Financial Analysts Journal* (March/April 2003):88–96.

Figure 1. Market Capitalization of the Largest 20 S&P 500 Stocks as a Percentage of the S&P 500, 1957–2003

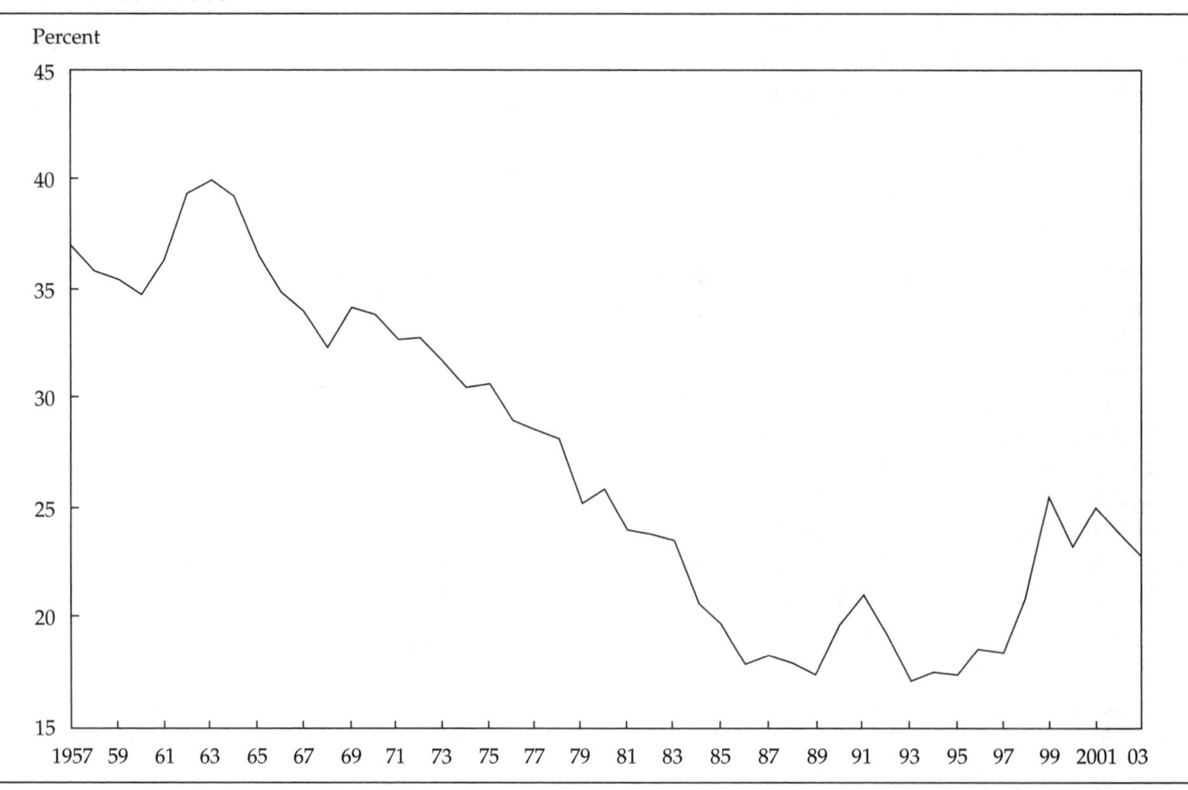

"Gaming," or buying in advance those companies that are new to a specific index (such as the S&P 500 or Russell indexes) while selling those that will be deleted, is clearly an important issue and all the more reason to buy the whole market, such as the Wilshire Total Market Index, rather than just a segment. But if investors wish to buy or sell different segments of the market, they will have all the problems, such as front running, that Gary Gastineau mentioned.[3] So, Peter is right that style indexes that are well advertised will have some extra costs connected with indexing to them.

A more important reason why straight indexing may not be as popular in the future is that investors should attempt to underweight bubble sectors, such as technology in 1999–2000 or oil in 1979–1980. The "efficient market" enthusiasts may scoff at the ability to detect bubbles, but I disagree. The underweighting of a surging sector could be the outcome of mean reversion in sector returns. I was not alone in calling technology valuations "uncalled for" in the last cycle, and although I was not willing to actively short those stocks (because no one knows when the bubble will burst), I and many others did underweight that sector.

[3]See Gary Gastineau's presentation in this proceedings.

Nevertheless, the indexing strategy remains a very attractive and viable option for investors if one is content to invest through all the cycles. Given the rather dismal long-run performance of active money managers and the extraordinarily small cost of indexing, I believe that indexing should and will remain popular.

Future Equity Returns—The Verdict of History

Historical evidence provides some clues to future return expectations. **Figure 2** is an updated display of my research into the past 200 years of stock, bond, and T-bill returns. The figure shows the total cumulative returns after inflation from January 1802 through 31 December 2003 for various asset classes. Interestingly, gold provided a cumulative return of only 39 cents above inflation over the past 200 years. This return should change some investors' minds about how much gold they should hold in their long-term portfolios, although many investors remain enthusiastic gold bugs in the short run.

It is the historical return for stocks, however, that strikes me as so important. The straight line through the cumulative stock returns is the best-fitted regression trend line. Notice how the actual stock returns cling so closely to this trend line. No other asset class

Figure 2. Total Real-Return Indexes for a $1 Investment in 1802, 1 January 1802 through 31 December 2003

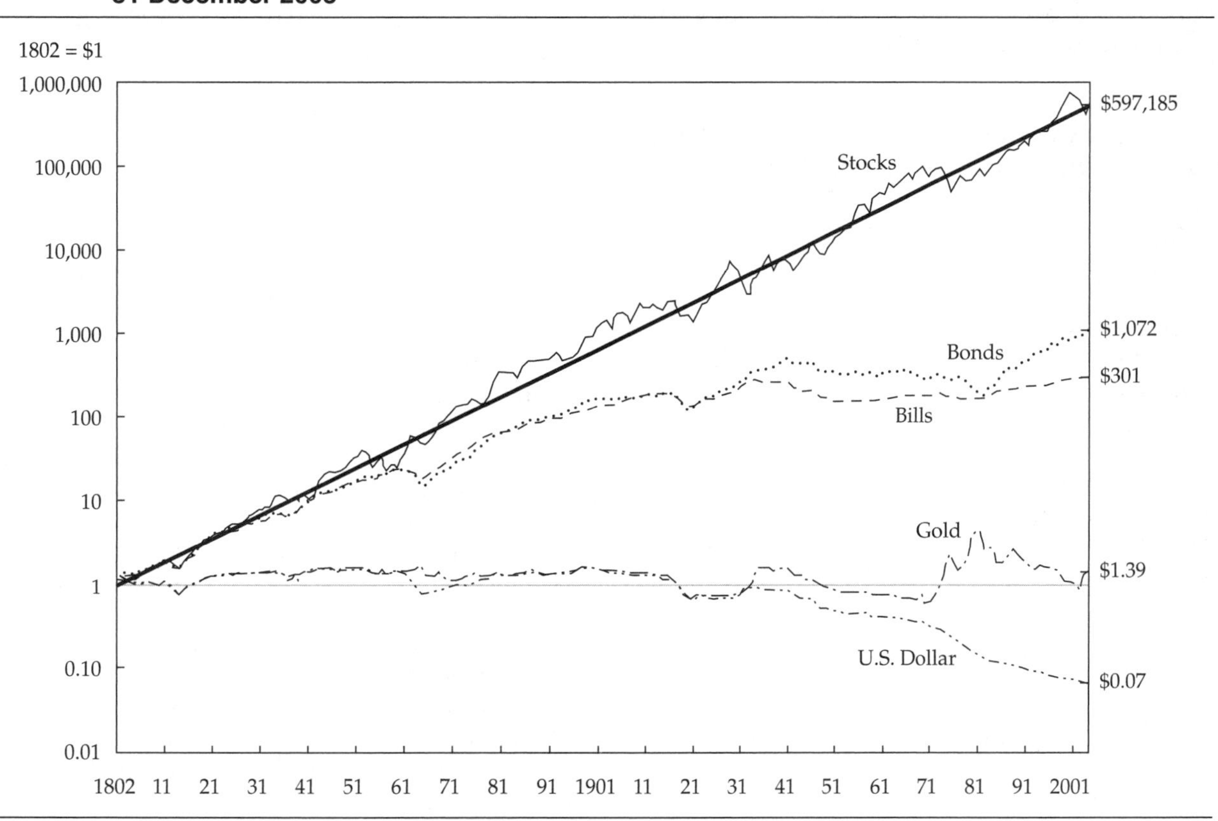

exhibits this behavior. Interestingly, in March of 2000, at the stock market peak, cumulative stock returns were 80 percent above this trend line. In the past, whenever the stock line went substantially above the trend line, investors were at risk because real stock returns are a mean-reverting process. At the bottom of the bear market, the market went 30 percent below the trend line, and it is now (February 2004) just about at the long-run trend line. If one considers the long-run trend line to be the fair market value, which I will look at again from a valuation standpoint a little later, the market is currently at fair market value.

The trend line for stocks represents a long-term real equity return of 6.8 percent a year, which Andrew Smithers and Stephen Wright called "Siegel's constant" in their book *Valuing Wall Street: Protecting Wealth in Turbulent Markets.*[4] Notice that at a long-term rate of 6.8 percent, an accumulation in equities with reinvested dividends almost doubles in purchasing power every 10 years.

Table 1 shows the total return for both stocks and bonds over the long run for three major subperiods and for several postwar periods. The 1802–70 period, for which the data for dividends are least reliable, offered an after-inflation equity return of 7 percent. Good dividend data starts in 1871, and the 1871–1925 period shows a real return of 6.6 percent. From 1926 to 2003, the "Ibbotson period," the equity return was 6.8 percent, and from the end of World War II to 2003, it was 6.9 percent. So, all the long-term returns fall between 6.5 percent and 7 percent, a remarkable confirmation of mean reversion.

Table 1. Stock and Bond Market Real Returns through 31 December 2003

Period	Stocks	Bonds
Long term		
1802–2003	6.8%	3.5%
Major subperiods		
1802–1870	7.0	4.8
1871–1925	6.6	3.7
1926–2003	6.8	2.3
Postwar periods		
1946–2003	6.9	1.5
1946–1965	10.0	–1.2
1966–1981	–0.4	–4.2
1981–1999	13.6	8.4
1983–2003	8.8	7.7

I do not need to remind most market participants that there can be substantial periods of time when real stock returns are not 6.5–7 percent a year. In fact, during the great bull market of 1981 through 1999, stocks had a 13.6 percent real return, which was exactly double the long-run average.

The bond returns shown in Table 1 are for government bonds. For the entire 1802–2003 period, the real bond return was 3.5 percent, which is about half that of stocks. And notice that real bond returns have gone down over time. For the 1802–70 period, the bond return was 4.8 percent; for 1871–1925, it went down to 3.7 percent; and for the 1926–2003 period, it was 2.3 percent. From the end of World War II until 2003, it was 1.5 percent. One of the reasons why the post–World War II bond return was so low is that during a 35-year period (1946–1981), bond returns, on average, were negative.

I hear a lot of individual investors asking whether the stock market might be entering a period like 1966–1981, when stock investors saw a real return of –0.4 percent. But no one asks me whether the bond market might be entering a long period of negative real returns, like what happened from 1946 to 1981. Although unlikely, negative real bond returns over extended periods are far more probable than negative real stock returns, and that certainly applies to today's prospects for bonds.

So, what do these data say about the equity premium? The long-run historical equity premium is much lower than equity premiums calculated from more recent data. From 1802 through 2003, the equity premium was 3.3 percent measured against long-term government bonds. From 1926 to 2003, it was 4.5 percent, and from World War II to 2003, the premium was 5.4 percent.

The equity premium has been increasing because real bond returns were biased downward in the post–World War II period. This situation occurred because individuals were pricing 30-year bonds in the 1950s and 1960s on the expectation of continued low inflation, which did not materialize.

Before World War II, the price level exhibited no overall trend up or down, so long-term investors projected little inflation. This trend was broken with the secular inflation of the 1960s and 1970s that devastated bond returns. Without a sudden surge of inflation, it is unlikely that real bond returns will be negative for such a prolonged period. But negative real bond returns over periods of 10 or more years are not out of the ordinary.

Projecting forward, I think the equity premium will be lower than it was in the period from 1926 to 2003 and certainly lower than the 5–7 percent that is often quoted in finance literature. But to determine future stock returns, the valuations of the market must be analyzed.

[4] Andrew Smithers and Stephen Wright, *Valuing Wall Street: Protecting Wealth in Turbulent Markets* (New York: McGraw-Hill Book Company, 2002).

Valuation of the Market

When it comes to current market valuations, pessimists abound. **Figure 3** shows the price-to-earnings ratio, or P/E, on stocks all the way back to 1871. And it shows the P/E calculated using both reported earnings and operating earnings. The P/E for reported earnings averages 14.8 over these 133 years and generally fluctuated between 5 and 25 until the last bull market, when it rose significantly higher.

Note that the P/E using operating earnings did not deviate much from the P/E using reported earnings until the late 1980s. Now, these two measures deviate quite a bit, particularly in recessions. Currently in February 2004, the P/E based on operating earnings is at 18.8 and P/E with reported earnings is at 22.8.

Concepts. Before diving into a discussion of comparing P/E measures using reported and operating earnings, a few concepts need clarification.

- *Operating earnings.* Operating earnings are too generous a concept and overstate true earnings. Operating earnings do not allow for option expenses and full pension costs, and they eliminate other costs that should be expensed.

Standard & Poor's (S&P) has recently promulgated a new concept called "core earnings," which has some very attractive features that correct for the deficiencies just noted.

S&P has estimated the difference between operating and reported earnings for every S&P company. The total bias suggests operating earnings are currently about 10 percent too high. Now, obviously, for some companies, particularly those in the tech sector, the bias is much higher because option expenses are higher. For other companies, however, the bias is much lower or nonexistent.

- *Reported earnings.* Although reported (or GAAP) earnings also do not include options and pension expenses, this measure has other downward biases and often *understates* true earnings. I do not believe that most of the write-offs of purchased assets should be included in GAAP earnings. S&P agrees, and these write-offs should be excluded from core earnings.

Huge write-offs are one reason why P/Es exploded over the past couple of years. Some write-offs, such as $100 billion in the AOL/Time Warner merger, raised the P/E of the S&P 500 by more than five points. So, be very wary of large write-offs distorting P/Es.

- *Other downward biases.* Other downward biases exist in GAAP and operating earnings. For instance, R&D is expensed when it should be capitalized, and this category is more important today than in the past.

Figure 3. Market P/E, 1871–2003

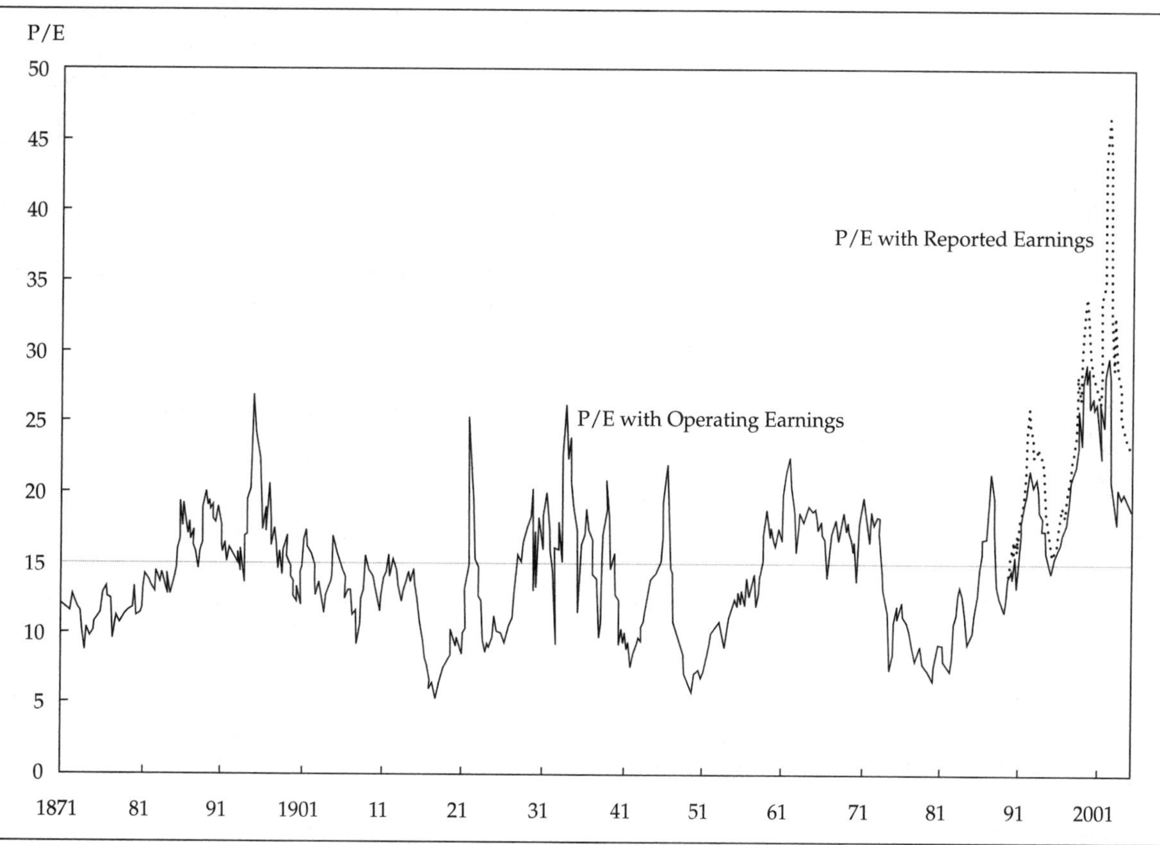

Another potential bias comes from expensing nominal and not real interest costs. In periods of inflation, the real liabilities of companies decline, but that impact is not accurately reflected in GAAP accounting. Inflation has been relatively low recently, so this has not been a big issue of late. But it was a huge issue back in the late 1970s and early 1980s because with the high inflation, companies had high nominal interest costs, which reduced earnings dramatically. But inflation was also lowering the real debt burdens of these companies. So, the expensing of nominal interest costs potentially creates another downward bias.

Current Estimates. According to S&P's website on 11 February 2004, the 2004 estimates for earnings on S&P 500 companies are as follows:

- operating earnings (bottom-up estimate), $62.72.
- operating earnings (top-down estimate), $60.74.
- reported earnings, $52.30, and about $7 of that is write-offs.

S&P estimates that $5.10 in current pension and option expenses should be deducted from operating earnings. So, I adjusted the top-down operating earnings estimate, which is a conservative figure, by the pension and option expense to yield a realistic number for forward-looking adjusted earnings: $55.64.

Because of the capitalization of R&D and inflation creep, one could argue that this number should be higher, but I will use $55.64 as a conservative estimate of the current ongoing earnings.

On 11 February, the S&P 500 was at 1,146, and with adjusted earnings of $55.64, the P/E of the S&P 500 comes in at about 20.60.

Equity Risk Premium. It is important to note that the long-term earnings yield (1 divided by the historical P/E of 14.8) is 6.8 percent. The earnings yield exactly matches the long-run real return. In theory, that is what is supposed to happen. Real capital is creating an infinite stream of real earnings. And the real earnings yield corresponding to a 14.8 P/E is 6.8 percent. The market is now valued at 20.6, which gives 4.85 percent for an estimated real prospective return on equities. This estimate is conservative, so accounting for some of the biases I mentioned earlier, I can round this number to 5 percent. This is the real return that the market is predicting given current earnings and current stock levels using the earnings yield as a return predictor.

As of this writing, indexed-linked bonds are at 1.7 percent for the 10 year and 2.1 percent for the 30 year. Standard nominal bonds are at 4.1 percent for the 10 year and 5.0 percent for the 30 year, but I will use the indexed-linked bonds because I am projecting real returns.

With a real return on equities of 4.85 percent and using the midpoint (1.9 percent) of the real return on bonds (1.7 percent and 2.1 percent), I get an equity risk premium of about 3 percent, which seems like the right level for the equity premium.

Rationale for Lower Equity Returns. Many wonder why the market P/E is higher today than its historical average of 14.8. Some suggest the P/E will likely move back down to its long-term average, and some say it may even fall below the average. I believe it should go back down to the average only if the economy and the financial markets are no different today, on average, from what they have been over the past 130 years—the years from which that average number is derived.

But I think some important differences do exist. First of all, the market is much more liquid and stock diversification is much easier to attain. How many investors in the 19th century and the first half of the 20th century had diversified stock portfolios? Very few. These investors were taking on much more risk, and they were rewarded with higher rates of return. But with the ease of diversification today, such higher returns are not warranted.

Something else leading to lower equity returns is the greater understanding on the part of the public about the equity premium. Investors are not going to find those "screaming gimmies" in the market like they could in the past. For example, in the early 1950s, blue-chip stocks had dividend yields of 7 percent and 8 percent and were well covered by earnings, but few investors wanted to own equities then. Investors poured into the 2 percent Treasury issue or 1 percent passbook savings account. They would not touch 8 percent blue-chip equities. Are we going to get back to that environment? I certainly do not think so.

Finally, the tax consequences of equity investing have become more favorable over time.

Thus, based on these reasons and others, I believe that a higher-than-average P/E on the equity market is justified in this environment.

Dividend Yield and Earnings Growth. Another way to estimate the forward-looking real return on equities is from a dividend discount model approach. A lot has been written about the fact that dividend payout ratios are currently low, in fact at record lows. Theoretically, a low dividend payout ratio should translate into higher growth of future earnings and dividends. In fact, for a given path of earnings, every 1 percentage point reduction in the dividend yield should produce a 1 percentage point increase in the long-run growth of earnings and dividends.

Table 2 shows dividend and growth data back to 1871 grouped into three time periods: the entire 133-year time period, the period before World War II, and the period after World War II. Notice that the average payout ratio has gone down dramatically in the post–World War II period as opposed to the prewar period. Before World War II, the average dividend yield was 5.07 percent; afterwards, it went down to 3.45 percent—a 162 bp reduction in the dividend yield. The postwar period also saw a 222 bp increase in the rate of growth of real per share earnings and a 100 bp increase in dividend growth. The reason dividend growth has not increased as much as earnings growth is that the payout ratio has gone down dramatically. That cannot be a long-run equilibrium. For a stable payout ratio, dividend and earnings growth must converge in the long run.

So, what is the current situation? How much will the growth in future dividends rise? The dividend yield on the S&P 500 is 1.6 percentage points lower than the postwar average. If, as theory indicates, the rate of growth of future dividends rises by the decline in the dividend yield, then the rate of growth of dividends should increase by 1.85 percentage points, the difference between the postwar average and current dividend yield. If one adds that 1.85 percentage points to the historical real per share earnings growth of 2.88 percent, the result is a 4.73 percent rate of real earnings growth. An important point is that investors cannot use the long-term average real growth of earnings and dividends to project the future because of the significant drop in the dividend yield.

Thus, my point prediction for future real earnings growth is 4.73 percent. If I add the 1.6 percent dividend yield to this number, I arrive at a 6.3 percent real return on equities going forward. If I conservatively assume that only half of the reduction in the dividend yield goes toward earnings growth, perhaps because management wastes 50 percent of the earnings, then I get a 5.4 percent real forward-looking return for stocks.[5]

Summary

This is a lower return world because the P/E for equities is justifiably higher than it has been historically, which implies lower long-term real equity returns. Siegel's constant of a 6.5–7 percent real equity return probably will not hold for all future periods. Investors probably will receive closer to 5 percent. Nevertheless, the real equity risk premium will still be roughly 3 percent. Investors will certainly seek other higher yielding real assets, but of the three major asset classes—stocks, bonds, and real estate—all are probably going to realize lower returns than their historical averages. Consequently, equities still offer an attractive premium for long-term investors.

[5]As an aside, I am in favor of paying out dividends because of moral hazard and agency costs. Doing so should reduce management's waste of shareholders' profits.

Table 2. GDP, Earnings, and Dividend Growth, 1871–2004

Time Period	Real GDP Growth	Real Per Share Earnings Growth	Real Per Share Dividend Growth	Dividend Yield	Payout Ratio
1871–2004	3.89%	1.64%	1.18%	4.50%	58.66%
1871–1945	4.51	0.66	0.74	5.07	66.78
1946–2004	3.08	2.88	1.74	3.45	52.06

Question and Answer Session

Jeremy J. Siegel

Question: Could you reiterate whether your data are arithmetic or geometric? Also, could you comment on how the average institutional investor interprets/misinterprets the equity risk premium vis-à-vis geometric versus arithmetic data?

Siegel: All the data I presented here are geometric, or compound annual returns. In my book *Stocks for the Long Run*, I also report the arithmetic returns.[1] I believe that most investors think in terms of the geometric return, although it is important to note that the capital asset pricing literature is formulated almost exclusively in terms of the arithmetic returns and thus risk premiums quoted in that literature are arithmetic.

Question: How does the increased leverage in the economy, notably the rapid rise in the total indebtedness at the national, regional, and personal level, affect market volatility?

Siegel: The increased leverage is measured against income levels, not against asset levels. Because asset levels have risen, there really hasn't been that much of an increase in relative indebtedness. Furthermore, interest expense relative to income has not risen.

And even if there were an increase in leverage, that is perfectly rational in a world where real economic instability has declined. All economists who study fluctuations in GDP, unemployment rates, industrial production, and so on report that the variance is going down. If the variance of the real economy is going down, it makes sense for companies and individuals to take on more leverage. Leverage is a function of the risk of the underlying asset.

A question I am often asked is: Why does the stock market seem about as risky as before if the real economy is actually more stable? I believe the answer is the increased leverage. As I just noted, this is a rational response to the greater stability of the real economy and will make stocks more risky than they would have been had leverage not increased. That is why risk in equities has remained constant—the offsetting effects of increased leverage and lower real risk.

Question: How can you compare price using estimated operating earnings with a historical price-to-trailing-earnings number?

Siegel: That is a fair question. When there is a cyclical recovery of earnings, as we are in now, earnings increases typically are 15–20 percent a year or more. But the steady state earnings increases are, in real terms, only 3 percent or 4 percent a year. So, using this year or last year in the P/E calculation makes only a small difference and does not change the overall picture.

Question: What type of real returns should we expect in the future if U.S. prospects regress toward the long-term world growth rate?

Siegel: Three British economists—Elroy Dimson, Paul Marsh, and Mike Staunton—answered that question well in *Triumph of the Optimists: 101 Years of Global Investment Returns*.[2] They examined equity returns in 16 countries over the past 100 years. What is very interesting is that when they did this international study, they thought the United States, with its very big returns, would be a outlier. But the United States wasn't on the top; it was fourth best in the group and only a little above the mean.

If you took a world index, the real returns on a world portfolio would not be more than 1 percent different from those of a U.S. portfolio. That is one reason why they titled their book *Triumph of the Optimists*. They said it surprised them how well equity prices did on a global basis. They claimed that after studying these 16 countries, they concluded that investors do not get materially the wrong impression by looking at U.S. returns (stocks, bonds, and T-bills). Certainly, stock returns have been a little bit higher in the United States, but historical equity returns around the world have been very high.

Remember that I am predicting lower future real returns on equities. Actually, I believe my point prediction for the United States is lower than what the average worldwide real equity returns have been over the past 100 years. In summary, the whole question of survivorship bias of U.S. equity data is not anywhere near as strong as many imagine.

Question: How can real EPS grow faster than GDP when historically it has never even matched GDP?

Siegel: First of all, theoretically, real per share earnings growth can forever grow faster than real GDP growth. If companies are not paying out dividends but instead buying back their shares, then per share earnings growth will be

[1] Jeremy J. Siegel, *Stocks for the Long Run* (New York: McGraw-Hill Trade, 2002).

[2] See Elroy Dimson, Paul Marsh, and Mike Staunton, *Triumph of the Optimists: 101 Years of Global Investment Returns* (Princeton, NJ: Princeton University Press, 2002) and "Irrational Optimism," *Financial Analysts Journal* (January/February 2004):15–25.

larger than real growth. It is true, however, that *total* earnings cannot grow faster than real GDP.

The total-earnings-to-GDP ratio must be stable, but per share real earnings can grow faster than GDP. There is no contradiction. Of course, if because of the recent tax cut or other reasons we go back to a 4 percent or 5 percent dividend yield (don't forget the average dividend yield between 1871 and 1980 was 5 percent), then per share earnings growth will drop significantly.

What I'm basically saying is if companies decide to keep dividends low, they're going to buy back their shares or use earnings in lieu of other equity or debt financing. This will reduce their interest costs and boost their future earnings growth.

Question: If write-offs are consistently reducing earnings, how can you disregard them?

Siegel: We all hear about write-downs. But has anyone heard about a write-up? There is an asymmetry in U.S. GAAP accounting. Let me give the following illustration. Suppose there are two companies, A and B. In a normal market, A buys B and that's it; they both stay at about the same price. But assume there is a bubble so that both A and B go up in price and then A buys B. Then, the bubble breaks so that both prices go back down to where they started. In this instance, GAAP accounting requires A to write down B by the amount of the decline in price. But is there any change from the example when A bought B and there wasn't a bubble? No. It is a portfolio write-down. Yes, I agree that A could have made a much better investment in the bubble (issue shares and hold cash, for example). But it is my belief that all those write-downs (particularly the AOL/Time Warner write-down) have nothing to do with forward earnings. Those write-downs do not affect the long-run earnings power of corporations.

Also, as I just noted, in GAAP accounting you rarely "write up" an asset. Companies have many assets on their balance sheet—land, copyrights, and so on—that have a value far in excess of book value. If these assets were valued today, they would be much higher than book, but that is not done. This is the reason why the S&P core earnings concept does not include write-downs of asset values.

Question: You subtract \$5–\$10 in accordance with S&P's core earnings adjustment for pensions and options, but you subtracted only from the operating earnings, not from the reported earnings. Shouldn't it be subtracted from both?

Siegel: Yes, that bias also exists in the reported earnings. But I don't think those reported earnings are indicative of the forward-looking earnings power of the corporation because of write-offs, so I do not use reported earnings when projecting equity returns or the equity premium.

Question: Jeremy Grantham says that bubbles rarely end without capitulation. What are your thoughts on that risk?

Siegel: Jeremy Grantham says that in a bear market there's always a move to below-average valuations. Well, we had the breaking of the bubble. We had a 50 percent price decline. I'm not saying that stocks could not go lower. But I think the market is pretty much at an equilibrium valuation now. If it does go lower, we should overweight equities.

In addition, as I mentioned, we are never, in my opinion, going to get those discouraged single-digit or even 10–12 P/Es that we had historically. People are just too smart in their asset allocation today. Sure, fear and greed and panic are always going to be emotions present in the market, but because of the liquidity and size of today's markets, we're just not going to get down to those low P/Es again.

Question: Is P/E still a valid metric given structural and accounting changes in the way we calculate earnings?

Siegel: We do need to address some of the questions of how we calculate earnings. I don't like operating earnings. There's no formal definition for it. I do think companies have abused operating earnings by overusing inventory write-offs and restructurings. Companies have said, "We didn't sell anything in this product line; let's just write it off as an inventory loss." Such actions are absolutely inappropriate. We should standardize our earnings calculations.

I was very encouraged when S&P started its core earnings project. But I have since backed off because S&P is calculating pensions in a way that I don't agree with. Nevertheless, we've got to improve reported or GAAP earnings. We must try to agree on a measure that represents the sustained earnings that could be returned as cash to shareholders.

Question: Shouldn't we all be paying more because volatility of markets, earnings, and dividends has collapsed as a result of increased sectoral diversification and diversification across stocks?

Siegel: The Chicago Board Options Exchange Volatility Index has been down over the past 6–8 months, but in the long run, there is no trend in the volatility of stock markets. I attribute that result to the increased leverage that companies have taken advantage of because the real economy has gotten more stable, as I mentioned earlier.

Question: If small/large and value/growth dichotomies are artificial, are you refuting the

Fama–French data that suggest small and value are riskier and, therefore, have a higher cost of capital and thus generate excess returns?

Siegel: They certainly appear to be an unexplained risk factor. We think they're hedging some sort of risk, but we don't know exactly what type of risk. It is clearly not the classical variance risk because that's why it doesn't fit into a strict capital asset pricing model.

What I was questioning was the way people are being asked to specialize. That is, do people naturally develop expertise in particular industries or in a particular type of stock? I can understand an industry specialization, which used to be the classical way of looking at stocks. But is the Fama–French distinction that we see today—small/large, value/growth—really natural?

Question: How do demographics and the pending retirement of the Baby Boomers affect your outlook, if at all?

Siegel: That's probably the biggest question not only for the next five years but for this century. Recently, Alan Greenspan said that the Baby Boomers are going to have their retirement benefits cut, and everyone reacts like this is news. We have known this for decades.

I've done some extensive research on this issue, and it is true that long-run returns could be quite negatively affected by demographics. But one promising avenue that could support equity prices is that the growth of the emerging nations—China, India, and elsewhere—could solve the problem because they have much younger populations. With projections of 6 percent GDP growth in developing nations (China is already at 8–10 percent and India has hit 6), these countries will be massive acquirers of financial assets from the developed world. In fact, they're also going to be supplying us the goods that we need for retirement. Basically, these countries will be exporting their goods to us, and they will be importing our assets to pay for these goods.

It turns out that in 10–15 years, China's economy will be bigger than the U.S. economy; by the middle of this century, China and India alone will be much bigger than all of Europe, the Americas, and Japan put together. So, these are going to be huge markets. Without going into a lot of details, asset prices will be significantly affected by this growth that is taking place in Asia. This growth makes me far more optimistic about the long-run outlook for equities.

Question: What do you see as the prospects for emerging markets as investments?

Siegel: You've got to look at the price of the asset. The prices of some of these assets are crazy, such as the Internet stocks in China. I think the growth of demand is going to be huge, and firms have to take into account where the growth of demand will be and then they have to have a global strategy.

Interestingly, over the past 30–40 years, countries that grew the fastest didn't have the best equity returns. There is a slight negative correlation between country growth and equity returns. One of the major reasons is that equity prices become overpriced in high-growth countries.

There are obviously some good values out there, and every U.S. firm and western firm has to pay attention to what's going on in emerging markets. But clearly, history has shown that caring only about growth and not price is a losing strategy.

The Future of Active Management

M. Barton Waring
Managing Director and Head of the Client Advisory Group
Barclays Global Investors
San Francisco

Success in the future means practicing safe, smart stock selection for a manager and safe, smart manager selection for a plan sponsor. Both need to begin with a clear idea of what beta is and what alpha is in the total portfolio; they involve very different expectations and very different risks and should be managed differently. Modern active portfolio or fund management must occur in the space of alpha versus active risk on the active efficient frontier. Successful active managers of the future, the ones the chief investment officer will want to pick, will have skill in forecasting alpha, will optimize their portfolios on the active efficient frontier, will be moving away from using the long-only constraint, and will have high breadth, good portfolio construction processes, low transaction costs, and stringent risk controls.

This conference has the term "points of inflection" in its title, and the notion that we are at a "point of inflection" and thus need to think differently about the policy portfolio has caused an interesting stir in the business. Because Barclays Global Investors represents many of the large pension funds and foundation endowments in the United States and abroad, my phone started ringing as soon as Peter Bernstein's piece came out.[1] One might have thought that his piece was an "emancipation proclamation" for traditional portfolio managers, freeing them from the undue burdens and constraints of benchmark-relative investing. In some ways, it was as if the children had been told that they could go out to the playground without adult supervision. A sense of euphoric expectancy was in the air: no more policy portfolio!

But alas, that is not to be. The policy portfolio, in fact, is here to stay, as is the necessary companion of the policy portfolio, benchmark-relative investing. And they are here to stay for very good reasons. Investment management is not, in fact, headed back to the undisciplined days that preceded the development of modern portfolio theory.

[1]See Peter L. Bernstein, "Points of Inflection: Investment Management Tomorrow," *Financial Analysts Journal* (July/August 2003):18–23.

Beta and Alpha in the Total Portfolio

To talk about either active management or the policy portfolio in a disciplined way, I have to start with an important discussion of how beta and alpha work together in a portfolio—bringing into the discussion the relevant aspects of modern portfolio theory.

As I go through this discussion, I will take the viewpoint of a chief investment officer (CIO) of a plan sponsor primarily but also of an investment management firm. As the CIO, I must consider the policy portfolio, which is in effect my total portfolio benchmark, and also the possibility of adding value to it through the search for active portfolio return. The thought process begins with the generalized capital asset pricing model (CAPM) as given by the following equation:

$$R_p = R_f + \beta r_b + \alpha \text{ (CAPM in ordinary algebra)} \quad (1a)$$

In the generalized CAPM depicted in Equation 1a, every portfolio's total return (and let me emphasize that this is true of *every portfolio*), R_p, can be broken down into three parts: first, the risk-free rate, R_f; second, a beta component times the risk premium for the market, βr_b; and third, an alpha, α, the residual return not explained by the market.

Following one convention for notation, lowercase r represents excess returns (in this case, returns above the risk-free rate), so it is a risk premium in the

CAPM sense of the term. Equation 1a uses r_b to represent the risk premium for a benchmark, although it could also be thought of as the risk premium on any fully diversified component of the market or even the market as a whole, which is most easily thought of as indexes of greater or lesser breadth of coverage. So, the equation is the risk-free return plus beta times a risk premium plus an alpha.

Note that this is essentially a regression equation. The CAPM framework (or at least the more generalized single- and multi-index models) can be thought about in many ways as simply a regression model. The important point about observing that this is a regression framework, and it is a point that I will return to later, is that beta and alpha are related but uncorrelated with each other. Every portfolio has a beta component and an alpha component. In the sense that beta really is about benchmarks that represent market returns, all investing is benchmark-relative investing! This is unavoidable. The protests from traditionalists notwithstanding, any and every portfolio can be and should be thought of as some combination of beta and alpha, and the obvious and useful consequence is that all investments must and should be done on a benchmark-relative basis. This should not be protested but embraced, and it is embraced by the best and most modern active managers and plan sponsors.

As the CIO of a sponsor, I am thinking about the CAPM version shown in Equation 1b—the multifactor or multi-asset-class version *implemented across multiple managers*:

$$R_p = R_f + \mathbf{w}_{\mathbf{mgr}}^{\mathbf{t}}\mathbf{B}\mathbf{r}_{\mathbf{b}} + \mathbf{w}_{\mathbf{mgr}}^{\mathbf{t}}\boldsymbol{\alpha} \quad \text{(multi-asset-class, multimanager CAPM version).} \tag{1b}$$

I must apologize for using vector-matrix notation to write this equation, because I realize that this notation is not accessible to everyone. The intuition, however, is not so hard. A portfolio is made up of, say, n different investment managers, and the sponsor is using k asset classes and styles to represent the desired beta exposures in its strategic asset allocation (SAA) policy. So, $\mathbf{B}$ is an $n \times k$ matrix of the n managers' beta vectors. To determine the effective total beta exposure vector across all the managers, the $(n \times 1)$ vector of manager weights, $\mathbf{w}_{\mathbf{mgr}}$, is transposed and multiplied by the $(n \times k)$ matrix of the managers' exposures to the k asset class and style betas. For example, if the fifth manager is 100 percent large-cap growth, the fifth row of that matrix would have 100 percent shown in the column representing large-cap growth. If a balanced fund manager were in the lineup, it might have a bit in almost every column. These are just the managers' benchmarks, or normal portfolios. By this vector-matrix multiplication, I am simply finding the collective beta exposure of the total of all the managers' individual beta exposures across the whole of the plan (i.e., I am calculating the effective asset allocation policy). Hopefully, it is close to the intended SAA policy. And likewise for alphas: The sum of the expected alphas across the n managers is obtained with the vector product at the end of the equation.[2]

So, the CIO of a plan sponsor effectively must add the betas and the alphas across all the managers, hoping to stay close to the SAA policy while still adding value. Despite the small amount of complexity in the addition of factors, this "real world" representation of the portfolio is still simply a version of the basic CAPM!

The basic CAPM is so important because the returns of the benchmark components (or more generally, the market portfolio) are all on the security market line (SML). This line graphically expresses the central idea of the CAPM framework in that it shows a linear relationship between beta and expected returns available from being exposed to the fully diversified markets. The SML teaches us that higher expected return means taking on more market-related risk, and conversely, taking on more market-related risk means higher expected return—not necessarily higher *realized* return but higher *expected* return. So, on the one hand, we say that *beta risk* is *unconditionally* rewarded: more risk, more return.

Here is the important distinction: Alpha, on the other hand, is only *conditionally* rewarded, and therefore, the expected alpha return is only conditionally different from its normal or unconditional expected return, which means that it will have a return of only zero percent! From the efficient market hypothesis, the unconditional expectancy for alpha is zero because the markets tend toward efficiency. The markets are a zero-sum game—a negative-sum game after fees and costs.

Under what conditions is alpha different from zero? The conditions that allow a positive expected alpha that are still consistent with modern portfolio theory are (1) some degree of inefficiency in the market plus (2) some extraordinary or above-average level of skill. Both factors must be present for the investor to have a positive expected alpha. The important conclusion is that, although we have to recognize that having a true expected alpha is one of the hardest things in finance (and, in fact, across all investors the average expected alpha must be zero), for the most skilled, a positive expected alpha can indeed exist.

[2] The portfolio can generate alpha in two ways—by selection or by timing across betas. Both forms are legitimate active-management disciplines. But if the portfolio is to have alpha, that alpha must be relative to a beta in some way.

Managers know that markets have to be inefficient to *some* degree to support a positive expectation for alpha. Often, that condition is inappropriately stated as both a necessary *and* a sufficient condition for seeking and obtaining alpha. It is, in fact, a necessary condition, but it is not a sufficient condition. Think of the most inefficient market imaginable—a hypothetical country with no equivalent to the U.S. SEC, no generally accepted accounting principles, and rampant insider trading and market manipulation. An index fund of even this highly inefficient market will still outperform half of the players (dollar weighted). Only the lucky and the skillful will beat the index. Luck is not a basis for a positive expectancy of alpha. Thus, because the players are playing against each other, positive alpha is not about inefficiency alone. Special skill is the final necessary ingredient. I cannot emphasize enough the need for this second ingredient, skill.

If a manager is working in a marketplace that is inefficient and if that manager has skill—if the manager can find those bits of information that have not yet been impounded in security prices and can trade properly on them, which is what skill is—then a positive, nonzero expected alpha can exist. We were not taught this in business school (in fact, in business school, the very phrase "positive expected alpha" might have elicited unpleasant comment from the faculty!), but this is the necessary and useful consequence of the fact that markets are not, in fact, perfectly efficient and that everyone's skill level is not, in fact, created equal (the business schools are right about their key point, by the way—on average, across all players, the expected alpha must be zero).

Another major difference between alpha and beta is that beta is almost free. Indeed, one very appropriate interpretation of an index fund is that it is a pure beta play. And we all know how little such beta exposures cost (to my firm's great regret!).

Positive alpha, however, is a rare and valuable thing, and generating consistent positive alphas is one of the hardest things to do in finance, especially after fees and costs.

So, beta can be thought of as the *efficient* component of the market and alpha can be thought of as the *inefficient* component of the market, a playground for active management. Managers should not charge alpha prices for beta deliveries—let me rephrase that: Sponsors should not pay their managers alpha prices for beta deliveries. Good managers are compensated for delivering alpha, not for delivering beta.

Framing Policy Questions for the Total Portfolio. Managers need a clear-eyed view of the beta and alpha structural components within their portfolios if they are to understand how their total portfolio returns are being generated. **Figure 1** frames the policy question for the portfolio in the fundamental dimensions of investment policy—expected return versus expected risk.

Figure 1. Illustration of Policy Questions for the Total Portfolio

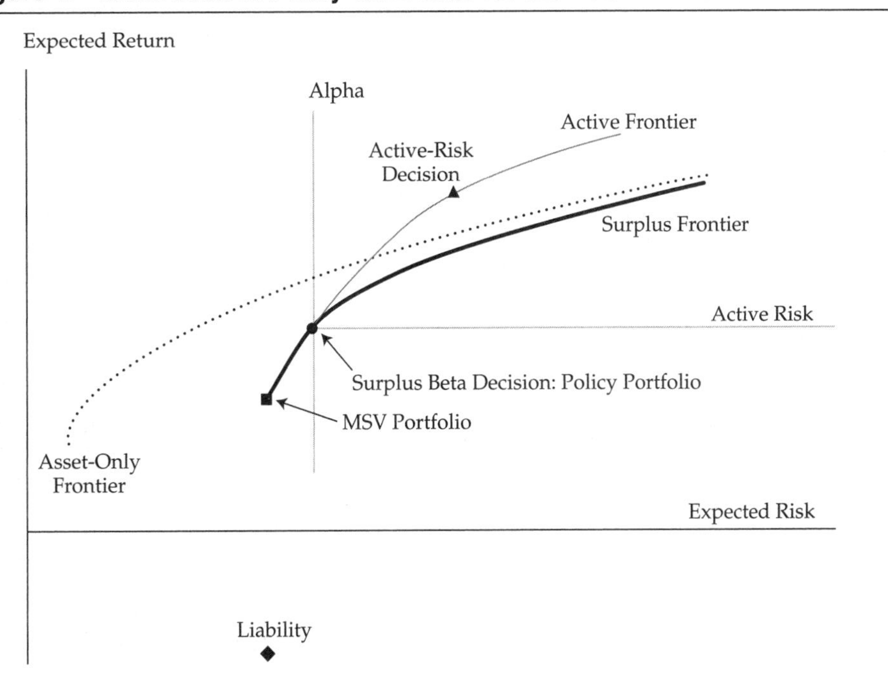

Note: MSV = minimum surplus variance.

We have to start with beta to set the stage for alpha. The long, upper-left efficient frontier in Figure 1 (the dotted line) graphs the well-known asset-only efficient frontier, which has been the basic tool for investment policy development and SAA for many years.[3] It has been the tool of choice for pension plans—public retirement plans, corporate retirement plans—and for many personal portfolios. Over the last 15 or 20 years, the typical pension policy portfolio has been moving from the left to the right (becoming more aggressive) to the point that it is now, on average, 70–75 percent equity, where earlier it was almost always less than 50 percent equity, and often much less.

But the asset-only efficient frontier is probably not the *right* efficient frontier for this purpose. A pension portfolio is expected to defease certain liabilities (indicated in the negative extension of the expected return space with a diamond). As for any other financial instrument or portfolio, the liability can be explained in terms of its beta or market-related components and its alpha components. But for this discussion, because the focus is on reducing the pension funding risk, consider the components of risk that the manager can hedge away. The idiosyncratic or alpha components of liability risk cannot be hedged away, so we need to consider only the beta or market-related components, which can be hedged away. These components can be modeled with asset classes or with other beta-type factors, and it is the return and risk for this portion of the liability model that we have plotted on this chart. Think of the liability as a special asset class, mixed of other asset classes (mostly bonds) and held short.

If the liability is a mix of asset classes held short, then the fully defeasing, matching policy portfolio of invested assets that would completely hedge that liability (in beta) would be the *same* set of asset classes as in the liability model, just held long. The net of these two positions would be a risk-canceling position in the sense that the beta risk to the surplus would be zero. This asset mix is plotted directly opposite to the liability model, reflected across the x-axis. This portfolio, in technical terms, is the minimum-surplus-variance (MSV) portfolio (shown as a square) and forms the lower-left end of what is labeled "surplus frontier."

It is a portfolio of assets that looks a lot like the liability. For example, in a narrow definition of liability, this portfolio is very bond-like; as a matter of fact, it would usually be heavily invested in TIPS (the common name for U.S. Treasury Inflation-Indexed Securities). A more inclusive and more forward-looking definition of the liability might include some equity-like risk. But regardless of the definition of the liability that is best to use (which is a conversation for another day), the MSV portfolio is some portfolio that would hedge away the diversifiable or market-related risks of the liability, the risks related to betas. Its net position across the combined assets and liability would have a sort of zero beta exposure to the markets relative to the liability, and it is in that sense that it is a minimum-risk portfolio.

Defined-benefit (DB) pension plans are in danger. More and more in the United States and in the United Kingdom, plan sponsors are struggling with pension investment risks, and there is some feeling that these plans are "out of control" in some undefinable sense. As a consequence, in the United Kingdom, almost no corporate DB retirement plans are left. Plans have been shut down, and companies have adapted cash-flow-matching policies for the remaining frozen plans. Being at a 70/30 (equity/bond) investment policy did not feel comfortable, and the alternative of cash-flow matching seemed more attractive. Australian plans faced this demon, and as a consequence, very few DB plans are left in that country. Of course, in the United States, sponsors are now facing heightened awareness of pension funding risks, and there have been threats that these valuable and socially beneficial plans may not survive.

So, if DB plans in the United States are to be saved, we as investment professionals assisting them in developing policy should help these plans apply better technologies to the management of the risks that are involved (i.e., we better find better approaches to building policy portfolios). Plan sponsors need a better understanding of how to set policy portfolio risk in the beta and alpha space so that the massive swings on the balance sheet, income statement, and cash-flow statement do not continue. And we, as the investment professionals that advise them, need to be "on a mission" to bring better tools to their management to help them survive.

Today, many DB plans are seeing their choice as one between their traditional, asset-only policy of 70/30 (stocks/bonds) and a cash-flow-matched portfolio. We recognize the latter as a special form of the MSV portfolio, the lower-left end of the surplus-efficient frontier. But choices are seldom binomial like this; there usually is a continuum of choice. And that is the case here.

A second more useful type of efficient frontier, the "surplus frontier," comes up and to the right from the MSV portfolio, asymptotically joining the asset-only efficient frontier as risk levels increase. This frontier provides the "connective tissue" between the most conservative investment policy, the MSV, and

[3]Remember, efficient frontier calculations should always use *forward*-looking expected returns, not *historical* returns. The past is not equal to the future in every dimension.

more aggressive investment policies. As an investor moves up to the right on the surplus frontier line from the MSV portfolio, he or she assumes a little bit more beta risk to the plan's surplus, and in contrast, a little bit more beta return. But as with the asset-only frontier, the slope of the frontier is declining as the investor moves up and to the right, and at some point, there is too much additional surplus risk that must be taken in the search for greater return, and that spot is the optimal policy portfolio, at least for the beta exposures that it is going to undertake.

So, it is not necessary to simply back off from taking any surplus beta risk completely and adopt an MSV policy, such as cash-flow matching. There is a continuum of choice. The surplus-efficient frontier is a readily available and well-understood tool for deciding how much market-related risk a pension plan should take in the search for market-related return, and it incorporates considerations of deciding just how well hedged one should be against the liability. Of course, plans should consider taking on some amount of beta risk—after all, market-related or beta risk is unconditionally rewarded with higher expected returns.

What does it mean in practical terms to take on beta risk relative to the liability? No surprises here; this is a way to "meter" out just how much equity exposure the plan sponsor wants. Equity exposures are legitimate and defensible. The question is: How much surplus risk is acceptable?

That question really is the issue, although many times the issue is framed in terms of contribution risk, or expense risk, or some such, but we can always trace these risks back to surplus risk. If the surplus is volatile "down," then to that extent, both contributions and expenses will be volatile "up." Everything traces back to surplus risk. If we control it, we control all other relevant pension funding risks.

So, although it is probably true that today's common policy portfolios of 70/30 equities/bonds are too aggressive for comfort in the pension plan arena, the choice is not a binomial one of simply abandoning the effort to set a chosen exposure to beta. The surplus-efficient frontier (which is created from technology that has existed for at least 15 years) shows us the path to a rational decision.[4] In 1988, Robert Arnott and Peter Bernstein published an article titled "The Right Way to Manage Your Pension Fund," which showed how, in a liability-relative view of investing, the relative riskiness of various asset classes changes.[5] Although they did not detail the technology for using this observation, that technology is the surplus-efficient frontier. This technology should be more widely used. It is a straightforward way of thinking about how much beta should be in a portfolio.

If the CIO completes this beta decision process and arrives at a policy portfolio that takes a conscious, intentional amount of beta risk relative to the liability, that portfolio will, of course, be on the surplus-efficient frontier, and suppose that it is at the round dot labeled "surplus beta decision: policy portfolio" in Figure 1.

So, with that dot (and the mix of asset classes that it implies) representing the beta aspects of policy, we have accomplished the portion of policy that historically has been thought about when SAA decisions are made.

But managing expected alpha and active risk is an additional dimension of investment policy that we can address today. Once the beta policy has been set, it becomes the benchmark against which *alpha* decisions are made.

Another set of axes can be drawn from the beta policy point (the paler axes) representing expected alpha (or expected residual return) and expected active risk (which is the standard deviation of alpha) relative to that policy benchmark. I will call this secondary graphical space "active space," or just "implementation space."

Can we separate the efficient frontiers in this way? Remember that when we think about the CAPM (or even a more general single- or multi-index model), it is a regression model, and so we know that true alpha is definitionally uncorrelated with the SAA benchmark and with any of its component asset classes. Thus, little or nothing is lost by using a two-step approach as I am suggesting here. The first step is deciding the portfolio's beta; the second step is deciding the alpha exposures.

The implementation space of alpha versus active risk is the space of modern active portfolio management. It is the space that *Active Portfolio Management: A Quantitative Approach for Producing Superior Returns and Controlling Risk* and other guidebooks on modern active portfolios use for building portfolios of securities.[6] It works equally well for building portfolios of managers, as I detail in the next section.

---

[4]It is not clear who first invented the surplus-efficient frontier, but Martin Leibowitz wrote a lot about surplus asset allocation and optimization in the 1980s. See, for example, "Total Portfolio Duration: A New Perspective on Asset Allocation," *Financial Analysts Journal* (September/October 1986):18–29, 77.

[5]Robert D. Arnott and Peter L. Bernstein, "The Right Way to Manage Your Pension Fund," *Harvard Business Review* (January/February 1988):95–102.

[6]Richard C. Grinold and Ronald N. Kahn, *Active Portfolio Management: A Quantitative Approach for Producing Superior Returns and Controlling Risk*, 2nd ed. (New York: McGraw-Hill, 2000).

Choosing Portfolio Securities or Managers. A CIO at a plan sponsor is an active manager. The securities that he or she chooses, however, are not individual or "atomic" securities but are aggregate or "molecular" securities, known more frequently as "managers." And this active portfolio of managers, like any other active portfolio, should be optimized by the sponsor with an objective function of maximizing expected alpha at some acceptable level of active risk.

When the CIO is assembling a portfolio of managers, he or she must first deal with the beta aspects because in current practice, most managers deliver their alpha with a designated beta—their benchmark beta. I mentioned earlier in this discussion that the weighted sum of the manager's benchmarks (it is a collective benchmark across the total portfolio then) must look closely like the intended beta or SAA policy. Although the historical betas are easy enough to measure, through regression, it is more important to have a *forecast* of the managers' forward-looking or neutral betas, the beta that, on average, can be expected in the future, the so-called normal portfolio. So, we know that as a part of any effort by the CIO to maximize the expected alpha from the managers, the betas need also to be accounted for, and in one form or another, the normal portfolio betas should be made to total to something close to the SAA policy. Think back to the points I made when showing the two versions of the CAPM earlier.

So, relative to the fund's surplus beta policy benchmark, the CIO can make an active-risk policy decision.[7] This second policy decision is made using the "active frontier" line, as labeled on Figure 1, coming up and out of the beta policy dot.

Of course, this line is upward sloping only to the extent that the sponsor selecting these managers has skill at picking managers—who, in turn, have skill at picking securities. Otherwise, this active efficient frontier would be flat or, after fees and costs, would actually be downward sloping; as I discussed, active returns are only positive conditional on skill.

Keep this active efficient frontier in mind during the rest of this presentation.

Optimizing. Optimization is, of course, the tool of choice for combining sources of alpha, just as it is the tool of choice for deciding the right combination of beta sources. The problem, like all other problems in finance, boils down to a trade-off between risk and return, in this case, expected alpha versus active risk, and optimization is how such trade-offs are resolved. Although optimization is growing to be more widely used for this task, in my experience, it is seldom used with sufficient control over the summation of the managers' normal portfolios and how it ties to the intended total portfolio's intended beta position.

Portable Beta. It is possible, once we have "connected the dots" with respect to the nature of alpha and beta, that we might have insights that change the way we think about building active portfolios. Historically, for example, when an investment manager sold an active investment management product, the product always was a "bundled" product with a component of beta and a component of alpha—for example, a large-cap value beta with an alpha. And it is safe to say that the fact that it was bundled was completely lost on the manager and on the client: Alpha and beta separability just was not part of the discussion. But, in fact, alpha and beta are independent. Alpha can be transported from one beta to another. A large-cap equity alpha can be moved to a bond beta. For instance, the firm Pacific Investment Management Company has a "stocks plus" product with a bond-like alpha that is moved onto a stock beta. Because the alpha and the beta components of the portfolio have different characteristics, they should be managed differently.

A great deal of research and work has been done on separating alpha and beta.[8] My group has long had software (available also to our clients) that helps organizations make decisions based on separating alpha and beta in actual application.

It has grown popular recently to use the term "portable alpha." I prefer to use the term "portable beta." Here is why: Recognizing that alphas are truly independent of beta, the CIO who believes in his or her manager selection skills should simply go out and hire the best sources of pure alpha, regardless of the betas that come with them, wherever they can be found. Then, the CIO can simply "fix" the betas by shorting the overexposed asset class betas and going long the underexposed betas. The beta is thus corrected to match the intended beta policy through these long and short "pure beta" transactions (such as futures, swaps, and trusts).

Of course, this is not really two separate steps. Because there are cost and availability issues when it comes to moving betas around like this, the two steps have to "talk" to each other in an optimization framework.

[7] For more on this topic, please see M. Barton Waring, "The Dimensions of Active Management," in *Improving the Investment Process through Risk Management* (Charlottesville, VA: AIMR, 2003); also, M. Barton Waring and Laurence B. Siegel, "Understanding Active Management," Barclays Global Investors *Investment Insights* (April 2003):1–40 and "The Dimensions of Active Management," *Journal of Portfolio Management* (Spring 2003):35–51.

[8] See, for example, Robert D. Arnott, "Risk Budgeting and Portable Alpha," *Journal of Investing* (Summer 2002):15–22.

In this sense, the generalized concept is really better named as "portable beta" rather than "portable alpha." The latter term suggests that the manager has to move alpha somewhere. But the manager does not; given that alpha is independent of beta, alpha has no requirement that it be connected to any particular asset class. So, "portable beta" is the full generalization of the concept of portable alpha.

Some commentators have suggested, with this idea in mind, that pension plans should be managed as if they were just giant hedge funds. To the extent that this means chasing true expected alpha skillfully, this, of course, can be true. But there are some important caveats.

First, unlike a hedge fund, the goal of a pension plan is not necessarily to have a zero beta. As discussed earlier, a plan sponsor should make a conscious decision about how much surplus beta risk to engage. Like a hedge fund, however, pension managers can seek the best alpha opportunities among all alpha sources, including hedge funds. But the pension portfolio is much more sophisticated than the typical hedge fund portfolio, which is not all that well managed and typically not net zero in its betas: The typical hedge fund is not a pure alpha play in most cases. Certainly, the sponsor can recognize a zero-beta hedge fund (such as a market-neutral, long–short fund) and will know how to fit it in with his alpha–beta separated portfolio in a sensible way. As I said previously, active management is hard, but with skill, it can be done—even by a sponsor!

Second, unlike a hedge fund, the pension plan's risk budgets for beta and alpha must be consciously set and rigorously managed. The benchmark must reflect the right portfolio objectives, and the ultimate benchmark against which both beta decisions and alpha decisions are made is the pension plan's liability. The risk–return trade-offs are ultimately viewed against that benchmark. A hedge fund's benchmark, by contrast, is often simply cash.

The well-managed pension fund strives to make conscious active-risk choices among the best alphas it can find. It is a difficult task. If the sponsor does not understand that hurdle of beating the benchmark before starting, the portfolio does not have much chance of winning. Facing that hurdle provides a reality check; good pension plan sponsors are modest about their skill at picking managers and finding and adding alpha: Adding alpha is hard. So, their active-risk budgets are not highly active, high-risk budgets. Typically, there will be *more* risk allocated to betas, which are unconditionally rewarded, than to alphas, which are only rewarded conditional on special skill.

The Future of Active Management

So, that is the "setup." Considering this big picture of the beta and the alpha working together under the direction of the sponsor, what might the CIO do in the way of picking managers on the basis of how they source alpha, and what might a portfolio manager do to pick securities and build them into a portfolio? What can we learn, and what do we already know about how to successfully manage the search for alpha?

First, let us manage some expectations. True expected alphas are much more modest in size than is usually believed. Sometimes, managers and plan sponsors frame their expectations for what they can do with some skill in terms of what they have seen done by others with particular bets. They hear all the stories—about someone who got out of technology stocks at the peak in 1999 or somebody who got into Xerox Corporation at the right time in the 1950s.

And in actual observation, we all notice that the average standard deviation of active return for active managers is 5.5–6.0 percent. So, a manager in the top 1/6th of skill level quite naturally expects to be up 5–6 percent versus his or her benchmark. These distributions of *realized* alphas seem appropriate for framing our expectations of *expected* alphas.

We can test whether this is a reasonable estimate for expected alpha by using the IC, or information coefficient, as a reference point. The IC is the correlation between alpha forecasts and the realization of those forecasts, so it is the key measure of active-management skill. A manager with an IC of zero has no skill; the manager's forecasts are meaningless. A manager with an IC of +1 produces perfect forecasts. So, the IC is a coefficient for the correlation between forecasts and realizations, and like any other correlation coefficient, it falls between –1 and +1, with 0 meaning no correlation.

Ronald Kahn's research, cited previously, indicates that the IC of a top-quartile manager is less than 0.05. In other words, it is not far from zero, on average. This IC can be interpreted as a manager being maybe 52–53 percent right on his or her calls, and 47–48 percent wrong. So, an IC of only 0.05–0.10 indicates truly exceptional levels of skill.

The correlation squared, the R^2, is a revealing number for our question. The R^2 is important because it reveals how much of the variance (the best measure of volatility) is explained by the active signal. For example, if the IC is 0.10 (very high by the scale of the prior paragraph), the correlation squared (the R^2) is 0.01, or 1 percent. The interpretation: Only 1 percent of active variance is explained by the signal by skill. The balance of active risk is just randomness or dumb luck! Most active-management returns are random;

they are not skill driven. So, it is not appropriate to drive one's expectations for alpha off the total range of realizations; 5.5 percent, the typical level of active standard deviation, is by no means a reasonable expectation for alpha. If one works through the math of variance with an R^2 of 1 percent, a more reasonable number might be 55 bps. There is more to this than I am glossing over, but the bottom line is that expected alphas are much more modest than we often think, and top quartile or one sigma or any other measure directly drawn from historical performance is not a good indicator for alpha expectations.

With such low ICs, separating randomness from skill is a challenge, so the CIO needs a mental model for active management. **Figure 2** shows the difference between the average participant in the market (or manager) and the skillful participant or manager with a positive expected alpha. The average active manager graphed in Panel A produces alpha that is normally distributed with a mean of zero (i.e., centered on the benchmark), less some amount representing fees and costs. On average, after fees and costs, the outcome is a negative-sum game plus the randomness necessarily created from the effort to add value. (I say that alpha is normally distributed. It is probably not normally distributed on any given day, but the central limit theorem says that over time, a distribution of any sort that is an independent and identical distribution will generate a normal distribution.)

Panel B shows what having a positive expected alpha means: With sufficient skill, the distribution will be shifted *up* to somewhere (hopefully!) above the benchmark. Returns are still highly random, and the distribution may be a little tighter, but the mean of the distribution, which is what is important, shifts up. The skillful manager will still underperform from time to time (and the unskillful manager will outperform from time to time). This is a useful model of skillful active management, representing both a nonzero positive expected alpha and the fact that most of the variance of active management is just random and not skill based. Notice that we can make a strong statement that alphas are distributed normally—forget about the "skewed" distributions some managers are fond of claiming.

Forecasting Alphas. By how much does the distribution shift? A good tool for forecasting alpha is the "Grinold equation" explained in *Active Portfolio Management: A Quantitative Approach for Producing Superior Returns and Controlling Risk*. The first version here, Equation 2, applies to a manager selecting specific securities:

$$e(\alpha_{security}) = IC_{mgr} \times \omega_{security} \times Z\text{-score}_{security}. \tag{2}$$

It states that the expected alpha of a security, $e(\alpha_{security})$, is equal to the IC of the manager (the manager's skill at forecasting stock returns) times the residual risk of the security, $\omega_{security}$, times the unit normal *Z*-score representing the manager's estimate of the true forward-looking mean return for that security, expressed in units of standard deviation within the framework of its own residual volatility.

The second version, in Equation 3, is from the viewpoint of a sponsor looking at managers:

$$e(\alpha_{mgr}) = (IC_{sponsor} \times \omega_{mgr} \times Z\text{-score}_{mgr}) \times \text{Efficiency} - (\text{Fees and costs}). \tag{3}$$

This is largely the same (the IC is now the sponsor's skill, and the *Z*-score is now the sponsor's evaluation of the manager's "goodness") but adjusted to meet

Figure 2. The Average Manager vs. the Manager with Positive Expected Alpha

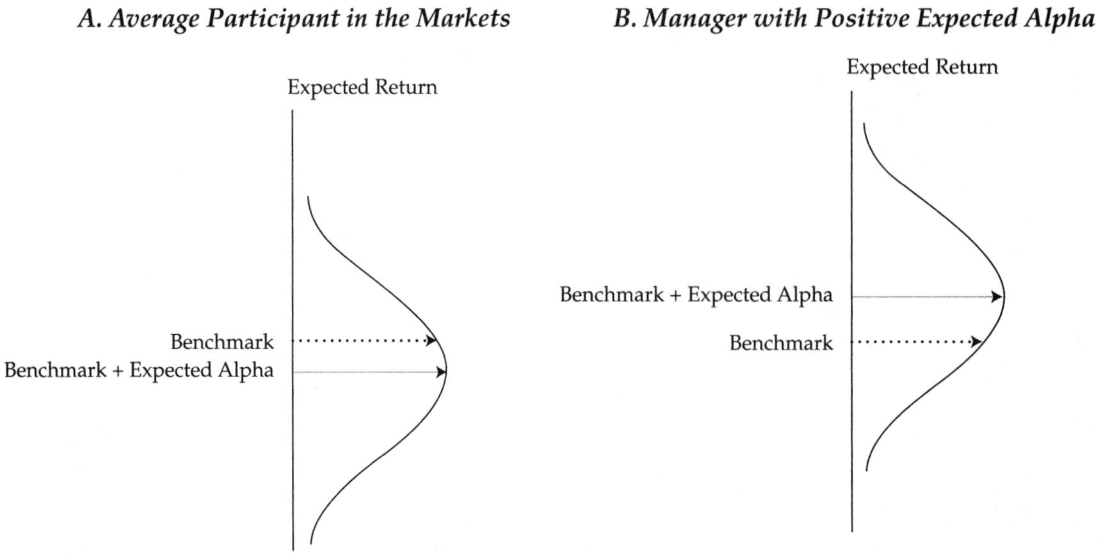

A. Average Participant in the Markets

Expected Return
Benchmark
Benchmark + Expected Alpha

B. Manager with Positive Expected Alpha

Expected Return
Benchmark + Expected Alpha
Benchmark

the sponsor's different situation with two additional terms. These additional terms are important and interesting. In addition to appraising all the managers, the sponsor must worry about their "efficiency"—that is, the expected alpha of the manager's implemented portfolio (probably a long-only portfolio) relative to the intrinsic expected alpha that the manager would have if operating without the shackles of the long-only constraint. This is discussed in more detail in the following section. The final challenge is that the sponsor must subtract fees and costs. After all, the sponsor's goal is to maximize expected alpha after fees and costs are considered. Because of these issues, especially the second concern over fees, a sponsor needs quite a bit more skill to be successful than the manager does. A sponsor probably needs an IC of 0.3 or 0.4 to be successful. As Kahn's work tells us, a manager needs an IC of only 0.05 or so to be top quartile, so in some sense, there is a bit higher challenge for the sponsor.

That load of fees and costs is a horrible thing. It tells managers that they better focus on delivering pretty high skill and thus consistent alphas if they want to earn their fees and cover the costs of active management. Sponsors are not going to pay a premium fee for long if they are not getting an alpha yield.

The Long-Only Constraint. I touched on this point earlier; now, I will cover it in more detail. The long-only constraint is probably the biggest and most important factor in producing inefficient portfolios, and in some ways, this point is one of the key points of this presentation.

Figure 3 shows the surplus frontier from Figure 1—expected alpha versus expected active risk. For the moment, I will consider it from the standpoint of security selection by the manager, not manager selection by the sponsor. In a world without constraints on long or short investing, a manager optimizing across alphas for individual securities would—conditional on skill, of course—face the efficient frontier represented by the solid straight line. But virtually all portfolios today are subject to a long-only constraint, and a constraint lowers any efficient frontier. So, the dotted line is the one that most managers face.

It is not just slightly lower than the unconstrained frontier; it is a lot lower. At 2 percent active risk, the efficiency of the constrained frontier is only 65–70 percent of the unconstrained efficiency. In other words, the amount of alpha captured per unit of skill at 2 percent risk is about 65 percent of what might be captured in an unconstrained world. That is a high cost to pay. It gets worse. At 5–6 percent risk, the efficiency is probably only 40–45 percent. At 20 percent risk, the realm of the concentrated portfolio manager (the 10-stock or 20-stock portfolios), the long-only portfolio is probably only about 15 percent efficient. These costs are huge just to pay for the luxury of being long-only.

The little secret here is that there is a way to be on the "better" efficient frontier, the upper one. The

Figure 3. Effect on Alpha from the Long-Only Constraint

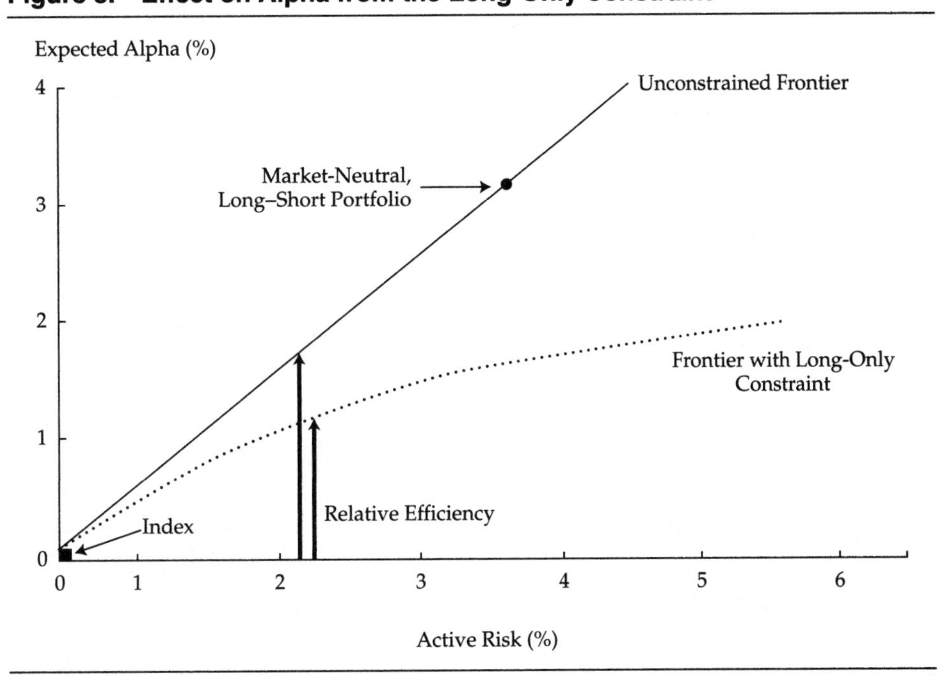

Source: Based on data from Richard C. Grinold and Ronald N. Kahn, "The Surprisingly Large Impact of the Long-Only Constraint," Barclays Global Investors *Investment Insights* (May 2000):9.

circle on the unconstrained (straight line) frontier marks a market-neutral, long–short portfolio, or what might be called an "unconstrained" portfolio (it needs to be under some constraints, but not a long-only constraint). For the manager who has insights, who has skill, the realm of market-neutral, long–short investing is a much more efficient place to capture alpha than the long-only frontier. (It is not quite as good as I have portrayed it because costs are associated with shorting; so, the circle may be down off the line a little bit, about 90 percent efficient.)

Long-only portfolios are probably here to stay for a long time because they have so much institutional inertia associated with them. But the lesson of the particular theoretical observation shown in Figure 3 is dramatic and important and will become even more so in the future: For those who think they have the best signal-gathering strength, the highest skill levels, getting away from the long-only constraint gives them a lot more product alpha to harvest and sell. For a given skill, there is a multiplied harvest of alpha. That is not only good for the ultimate client, but it is also good for the managers because more alpha usually means better fee revenue.

What is the intuition behind this issue? The long-only constraint is such a problem because it discourages managers from using research insights in a selling discipline. **Figure 4** depicts a distribution of signals—from strong sell to strong buy—in a (nonrigorous) normal distribution. Managers spend most of their time on the right-hand side of this curve with their "buys" and "holds." In a long-only universe, managers do not even attempt to put their knowledge and skill to work on the left-hand side. If they try, they quickly run into the long-only constraint: They can sell down only to a zero holding of any security, and not below that.

Any organization that has skill at getting alphas has the ability, conceivably, to use the same set of insights to make sell decisions as to make buy decisions. A good signal-generating insight has as much value on the left-hand side as the right-hand side. So much is wasted when left-hand-side insights cannot be chased and thus are not even given the same level of attention as right-hand-side insights.

As stated earlier, a manager who is subject to the long-only constraint can sell down only to a zero weight. That point is not far in a broad-cap universe. For example, for the S&P 500 Index, a manager can sell down 1/500th, on average. (Averaged by name, it is actually much less.) The loss of the entire left-hand side of that spectrum of signals is the source of the loss in the long-only constraint. So, the CIO of tomorrow will be paying more attention to a manager's selling discipline. At my firm, we have put a major stake in the ground around this idea, putting much of our product research and development budget into this area. It is no accident; it is the future of active management.

Breadth. Other important ideas are shaping the future of active management. Another aspect that will be important to portfolio construction in the search for alpha in the future is breadth. Breadth is the number of independent decisions a manager makes in a year. The square root of breadth times the IC (i.e., skill)—and for the long-only manager, times efficiency—produces the information ratio (IR):

$$\text{IR} = \text{IC} \times \sqrt{\text{Breadth}} \times \text{Efficiency}. \qquad (4)$$

Narrow breadth in a portfolio wastes alpha for a given amount of skill. A positive, nonzero skill number (evidenced by an IC greater than zero) is needed to have a positive expected IR, but sufficient breadth is also required if that IR is going to have much size to it.

Figure 4. Long-Only Constraint's Impact on a Manager's Opportunity Set

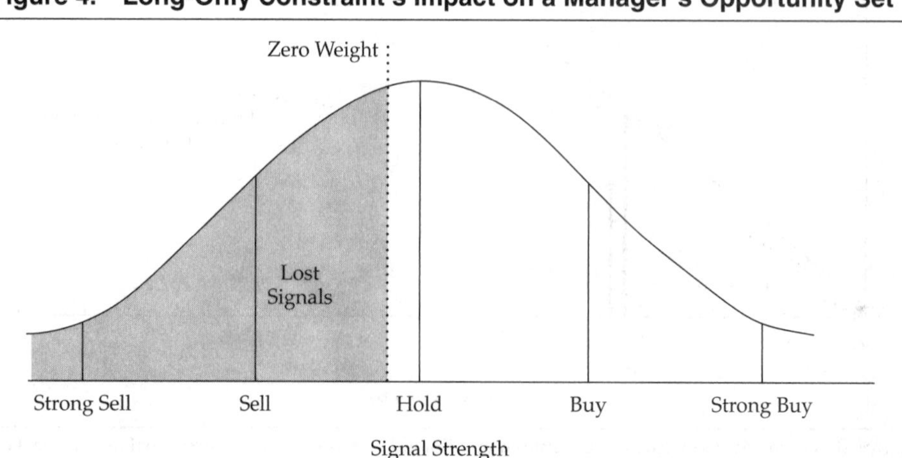

Narrow breadth, resulting in low IRs, is the reason traditional approaches to tactical asset allocation (TAA), even if skillfully implemented, have had long runs of poor performance and long runs of great performance. Some of these strategies have had quite strong ICs, but because of low breadth, they delivered inconsistent performance (low IR). Because of Equation 4, modern approaches to TAA involve many asset classes, subasset classes, and sectors. The modern asset allocator is making every effort to increase breadth. For example, our researchers have increased breadth in this category up to the area of perhaps 100 and are still working on increasing it. Other sophisticated organizations are following the same path.

A concentrated portfolio of securities also has narrow breadth, which makes maintaining a consistent IR difficult. The result is that managers of concentrated portfolios (including style-based portfolios) are fighting against headwinds. One needs an extraordinarily high IC to be a good concentrated manager because of the narrow breadth. A sponsor needs to be quite skeptical of track records for low-breadth strategies. As always, in understanding good performance, a lengthy track record is required to differentiate luck from skill. Low IR strategies will take longer to produce statistically significant *t*-tests than will high IR strategies.

Again, for a given amount of skill, look for higher breadth over lower breadth. Lots of small bets are better than a few bigger ones.

Portfolio Construction Processes. Poor portfolio construction processes also waste alpha. When building active portfolios, the CIO and the manager today need to optimize against a benchmark. The old approach of holding equal-weighted or modified-equal-weighted portfolios is demonstrably suboptimal and implies wildly divergent expected alphas.

Optimal security weights are benchmark weights plus or minus a signal-driven "active weight." Today's world is a benchmark-relative world. The traditional portfolio manager goes out in the field and fills up his or her basket with pretty flowers—the prettiest flowers he or she sees in the field. The modern portfolio constructor building alpha portfolios goes out with a basket that already holds every flower in the field in proportional quantities and modifies the basket by throwing out a few of the less pretty ones and adding a few of the prettiest ones. We know from other mathematical insights that in the optimal portfolio the highest active weights should be given to the strongest signals with the lowest risk. This approach maximizes the power of the insights, the alphas, the manager has.

Equal-weighted portfolios are never optimal, but we still see a great many equal-weighted portfolios out there—and for that the benchmark-relative optimizers are grateful.

Transaction Costs. Poor management of transaction costs also wastes alpha. Everyone must be intense about squeezing excess trading costs out of the portfolio. Alphas are rare, and they are modest in size. They must not be subsumed by trading costs—commissions/spreads, market impact, and opportunity costs.

Trading costs in some sense are a measure of alpha. An equilibrium probably exists between alpha and the trading costs of capturing it: The people on the trading floor, the specialists and the like (and even the brokers), are always thinking about the information that a manager might have when the manager is trading against them. So, in a very real way, they are pricing the manager's signals even as they push against the manager with market impact costs.

Market impact costs, although they are unobservable and very difficult to study, are very real and must be acknowledged and dealt with. Indeed, they are much larger than most organizations acknowledge. Traditional portfolio managers often still say their total market impact costs are included in the "spread," which is about 35 bps. It is not true. It cannot be true. Total trading costs for a typical traditional manager are almost certainly greater than 1 percent a year and probably a fair bit higher (maybe 35 bps of explicit commissions and spreads for a U.S. equity manager plus 50–125 bps of additional market impact costs, depending on which academic study one thinks is most accurate).

So, the bottom line is that trading costs, properly viewed, can eat up a lot of hard-won alpha. They should be subject to the tightest, most intense management that can be mustered.

Risk Controls. The first rule of active management is to take no uncompensated risks. Poor risk controls waste alpha. A good model for controlling beta risk, such as the Barra model (although there are others), is absolutely necessary. As a manager, you do not want to buy both Ford Motor Company and General Motors Corporation just because you like them individually; you will find yourself overweighted in the automobile sector where (if you had thought about it) you would have perhaps wanted to be neutral. This type of decision is the realm of risk controls—squeezing uncompensated bets out of the portfolio.

Skill is not a substitute for risk control. If it is to be taken, any active risk must be *compensated* risk, and it must be driven by a signal that the manager intends to make a bet on. The "accidental" risks that creep into a portfolio as by-products of skillful insights but that are not related to those insights are not compensated, and they need to be reduced to a minimum. This requires excellent risk-control technology.

Conclusion

The best results for active managers going forward will be driven by a clear-eyed search for true alpha in portfolios characterized by wide breadth, optimization of alpha, risk controls and risk budgets, low transaction costs, and no long-only constraint.

The approach is constrained in that stringent beta risk controls are needed, but these are sensible controls on how much beta should be taken, and the benchmark for this beta should be set relative to the liability.

Gary Brinson showed in his famous series of studies in the 1980s that, *on average*, managers do not add value for sponsors.[9] That it is only the most skillful managers who can add value is a truth that managers need to deal with. So, the challenge for managers is to have a more focused and clear-eyed view of how to add alpha. If managers are going to play the game, they must understand the rules of the game and must be able to take advantage of the navigation aids that can help them.

To highlight this thought, the best managers will observe these process ideals:

- a clear focus on generating pure alpha (not hiding behind beta),
- wide breadth,
- aggressive management of transaction costs,
- optimized portfolio construction,
- aggressive reduction of uncompensated risks,
- formal risk budgets, and
- either low-active-risk levels in long-only portfolios or any (targeted or budgeted) active-risk level in market-neutral, long–short strategies.

The less-than-best managers will be those taking high active risk, which leaves them facing a double problem—low efficiency (a low expected alpha harvest) at the hands of the long-only constraint and high risk, which reduces their optimal allocation in the sponsor's portfolio. I mentioned earlier that the optimal portfolio of managers in the sponsor's portfolio is held in proportion to their expected alpha divided by the variance of their active risk, or risk squared. So, for a given level of expected alpha, the higher risk, because it is squared, means a *much* lower weight in the portfolio. Managers with poor methods for portfolio construction and for controlling uncompensated risks will thus be wasting a good portion of whatever insights they have, in the sense that the excess risk they take on will reduce their attractiveness to sponsors.

There is a convergence here between long-only active managers and hedge funds. Hedge funds will also be applying more risk controls, and more importantly, they will be moving toward market-neutral, long–short approaches. One would think that hedge funds should already be adept at market-neutral, long–short portfolios, but they have traditionally done a poor job of squeezing all the beta risk out of their portfolios. For example, Stephen Brown and William Goetzmann noted that most hedge funds are net long in beta and have an average alpha not statistically different from zero.[10] So, the end result is that all forms of active management will increasingly be drawn to that carefully beta-controlled market-neutral long–short form of portfolio organization.

If you are the CIO of either a sponsor or an investment manager or are aspiring to be one, you need to think about the principles and approaches I have described. For most traditional organizations, it will be a change from what has been a more or less seat-of-the-pants way of operating, and few people like change. Change means learning new techniques, doing things differently and outside of one's personal comfort zone. But success in the future means practicing safe, smart stock selection by managers and safe, smart manager selection by sponsors. Today's CIO may not be comfortable with the mathematical aspects of controlling a modern active portfolio, but it is only under informed leadership by a knowledgeable CIO that these portfolios will thrive.

[9]See, for example, Gary P. Brinson, L. Randolph Hood, and Gilbert L. Beebower, "Determinants of Portfolio Performance," *Financial Analysts Journal* (July/August 1986):39–44.

[10]Stephen J. Brown and William N. Goetzmann, "Hedge Funds with Style," *Journal of Portfolio Management* (Winter 2003):101–112.

Question and Answer Session

M. Barton Waring

Question: Are conditions in place that would allow sponsors to adopt a long–short strategy?

Waring: Yes, conditions are in place. Many plan sponsors have guidelines that prohibit shorting, but in most cases, those guidelines were adopted by the board and the board can change them. Other guidelines are written in a way that exceptions can be made on a case-by-case basis. Many plans have some flexibility—either a particular exception to the long-only constraint or a provision for redrafting the rules themselves in the future.

Plans that are subject to statutory restrictions and have other problems can be inflexible (as those of you who have dealt with legislative politics around investment policy are aware). Public plans are most likely to have this problem, and corporate plans are least likely.

Question: Do you see an inconsistency in prescribing wide breadth when Peter Bernstein is suggesting that investors use a no-cut, five-year contract and that research adds value and trading costs are bad?

Waring: The reason you need some longevity to positioning is more about beta bets than about alpha bets. Alpha bets tend to have a relatively fast cycle, but beta positioning is more long term. For example, if you are betting that value is going to outperform growth over the next five years, it would not be fair for a sponsor to hold you accountable to that bet on a year-by-year basis. Those kinds of returns are slowly realized.

Beta bets are a legitimate active management discipline. Beta bets and TAA have gone out of favor because success with TAA is difficult to accomplish with a given amount of skill but a narrow-breadth strategy. But TAA is, in fact, a legitimate active-management discipline. Insight on beta bets is as valuable as insight on any other bets, especially if you have enough breadth to diversify your bets.

Breadth is a diversification issue. Beta bets, like any other active bet, tend to have low correlation, so the more you have, the lower the risk in a portfolio. Any way that you can put breadth into the portfolio is important.

Question: How should one adjust for the fact that betas in alpha portfolios are inherently unstable?

Waring: All returns are unstable in terms of *realizations*. Expectations are one thing; realizations are another. Realizations are drawn from the standard deviation around the expectation, and we tend to have portfolios that have a higher standard deviation in beta than in alpha—about 9 percent for beta's standard deviation and maybe 1–2 percent for alpha. To that extent, of course, realized beta is more unstable.

Another way of interpreting the data, however, is to remember that finding of Brinson et al. that 90 percent of the variance we take is on the beta side—on the SAA side—not on the active side. What that fact means is that because that risk is compensated (it is on the SML), it generates an *unconditional* expected return. Taking that sort of risk is more *comfortable* than taking the risk for which we have to put our skill on the line—that is, alpha risk. With alpha risk, if you are a sponsor, your skill at picking managers is on the line. If you are a manager, your skill at picking securities is on the line. Because we are more comfortable about taking beta risks, our portfolios are more unstable in beta, which is natural.

Question: Can you use an optimization approach when constructing a fund-of-funds hedge fund?

Waring: This question goes to the very heart of some issues with hedge funds today. Hedge funds are not transparent (although that aspect is improving); they tend to be net long in beta, and moreover, their betas are hard to determine. If we really wanted to optimize a hedge fund fund of funds, we would optimize the true alphas against the true active risks, thus correcting for whatever forward-looking net betas (normal portfolios) were in the fund so that we could have an *intentional* beta when summed across all those products—or at least have an *understandable* beta, one that we might fix or incorporate properly in our portfolio. We don't have the ability to do that because for hedge funds and for funds of funds, no good benchmark typically exists.

The problem is not that betas aren't in the fund. It is simply hard to sort them out or ferret them out. So, we end up with an *ad hoc* process of including hedge fund funds of funds in our optimization. We probably should be trying to optimize them in accord with the right principles, if nothing else, "in our heads." We would have at least a *fuzzy* optimization. If you have a feel for what's going on with optimization, you don't have to crank the handle on a mean–variance optimizer to get an optimized result; you can do it in your head. This is better than nothing when the inputs for a formal optimization are unclear.

Traditional Indexing Is Passé

Gary L. Gastineau
Managing Director
ETF Consultants, LLC
Summit, New Jersey

Indexing today is, in some regards, quite different from what the founders of indexing had in mind. Although the differences are not surprising, they have resulted in problems for investors who use indexes. Fortunately, the problems are not insurmountable and can be remedied by doing such things as adopting silent indexes, creating buffer zones to reduce turnover, getting rid of capitalization-weighted indexes, and abandoning the asset benchmark. But perhaps above all, contrary to the ideas of the indexing founders, active management can add value to index funds.

The word "passé" means a number of different things—slightly obsolete or obsolescent, inefficient, inappropriate, and so on—all of which are appropriate for describing traditional indexing in today's investment environment. In this presentation, I will discuss traditional indexing and the problems that make it passé. I will then address some ways to remedy these problems.

Vision of the Founders

One view of traditional indexing comes from the founding fathers of indexing. For those who have not read it, I strongly recommend Peter Bernstein's chapter "The Constellation" on the founding of indexing in his book *Capital Ideas: The Improbable Origins of Wall Street*.[1] It is an extraordinarily good description of the original ideas behind indexing. The central idea was that an index fund would be a portfolio product with low fees. The indexing founders were also looking for low turnover and low market impact associated with informationless trades. And they were looking for broad diversification. Essentially, their goal was to have the entire investable market in one "unmanaged" portfolio. Basically, the founders wanted to avoid the costs and mistakes of portfolio managers because some of the early proponents of indexing were adamant that the portfolio manager did not add value.

Like most ideas that have been influential, a number of things have happened in subsequent years that have made a few of these ideas seem a little bit naive. I think it is fair to say that indexing, as it is practiced today, is different in a lot of respects from what was in the minds of the indexing pioneers.

Today's Index Funds

By and large, today's index funds do have low fees—at least the most successful funds do. To the best of my knowledge, no billion dollar S&P 500 Index fund has an expense ratio of more than 1 percent, which is a relatively low fee in the mutual fund world. Thus, consistent with the ideas of the founders, index funds are still managed to achieve the objective of low cost, although considerable differences in fees exist among index funds.

One highly variable component of costs is turnover. Turnover ranges from less than 10 percent in some of the broad market indexes to more than 40 percent in some of the growth and value funds. The higher turnover comes from periodic rebalancing of growth and value funds and the fact that the criteria for determining growth and value often lead to frequent categorization changes. Even among the broader market indexes, the Russell 2000 Index is notorious for having an extraordinarily high rate of turnover. So, a number of funds that embrace the indexing idea do not have the low turnover that the pioneers conceived.

Diversification has been a bit eclectic in some index funds. The broad market index funds have generally worked as designed, although again, turnover and the costs of that turnover have been high.

[1] Peter L. Bernstein, *Capital Ideas: The Improbable Origins of Wall Street* (New York: Free Press, 1993).

Style indexes (e.g., growth and value) have high turnover but decent diversification within the style categorization. Sector funds (e.g., energy and technology) are less diversified and tend to be special purpose funds. Company-size-based funds (e.g., large cap, mid cap, and small cap) have generally worked well—given the limited range of what they purport to accomplish.

The concept of unmanaged index portfolios is interesting because the degree of management that has taken place in index funds has varied greatly from one index fund to another and from one index to another. The first index that was used successfully in broad market indexing was the S&P 500, and Standard & Poor's has always had an active index committee. The S&P index committee is why one often hears S&P 500 funds collectively called "the largest actively managed fund in the world." Because S&P's index management is an active management process, I do not think the funds based on the index can be described accurately in any other way. The S&P index committee does have policies, but it has also made a number of decisions over the years that have led to a high level of turnover and a high level of transaction costs.

The idea of not having "management" of an index fund is a bad idea when taken to the extreme. An index fund manager can add value, so the idea of active management in an index fund should not be completely shunned. The active management may be nothing more than varying the time when a change in the index is implemented in the fund; a simple timing change can add significant value. Another active-management possibility is an optimization process that uses less than all the stocks in the index, which can result in lower transaction costs. Keep in mind that the embedded transaction costs associated with an index, and with the funds that use that index, tend to increase with the popularity of the index. In an article I wrote in 2002, I examined the ability of some index funds to perform better, even after expenses, than their underlying index.[2] In many cases, active management of index composition changes by the index fund manager can lead to considerable performance differences with negligible risk of negative index tracking.

A recent article by Edwin Elton, Martin Gruber, and Jeffrey Busse addresses the issue of effective index fund management.[3] They took the universe of all S&P 500 index funds with the exception of exchange-traded Standard & Poor's Depositary Receipts (SPDRs), which they analyzed separately.[4] For a six-year period, 1996–2001, they calculated the difference in performance for the various funds. They found a significant difference, more than one might expect, between the best-performing S&P 500 index fund and the worst-performing S&P 500 index fund over that period—an annual rate of return difference of 209 bps. These are index funds. They are usually described as being commodities, but a 209 bp annual performance difference existed between the best and the worst over a six-year period. Obviously, part of the cause for this difference is expenses. Not everybody charges as little as the Vanguard Group, for example, to run S&P 500 index funds. But expenses do not account for all the difference. Some of it results from variations in the way different firms approach managing an index fund.

With that kind of performance difference on the most commoditized of all types of index funds, one needs to think a little bit about what kind of value an index fund manager can add and what can be done to better construct an index fund.

What Makes Today's Funds Passé?

Some features that were not anticipated by the founders make today's index funds passé. First of all, contrary to the founders' ideas, the most popular indexes, the S&P 500 and the Russell 2000, were not designed as efficient portfolio templates. They were designed as benchmarks or as a way of describing what was going on in the market. In that context, they have features that make them particularly inefficient as portfolio templates.

In addition, and perhaps most important, is the fact that with a benchmark index fund, the world knows what the manager has to do to trade in his or her portfolio when a change occurs in the composition of the index. Thus, everyone can trade at the same time the manager does. So, in effect, the index manager is providing information on the fund's transactions in advance. I do not know of any active fund manager in the world who would agree to a situation where trades were announced in advance. It simply makes no sense to run a fund that way.

In the early days, nobody thought that indexing was going to get to the size where changes in the index and the implementation of those changes would have the enormous effect they have now. As a result, there is active front running of index composition changes today. In fact, a cottage industry, or perhaps more than a cottage industry, has emerged that tries to

[2]Gary L. Gastineau, "Equity Index Funds Have Lost Their Way," *Journal of Portfolio Management* (Winter 2002):55–64.

[3]Edwin J. Elton, Martin J. Gruber, and Jeffrey A. Busse, "Are Investors Rational? Choices among Index Funds," *Journal of Finance* (February 2004):261–288.

[4]For the analysis of SPDRs, see Edwin J. Elton, Martin J. Gruber, George Comer, and Kai Li, "Spiders: Where Are the Bugs?" *Journal of Business* (July 2002):453–472.

determine the next changes in the S&P 500 and the Russell 2000. This is a very active market; hedge funds do a lot of this kind of trading. So, to the extent that people other than S&P 500 index fund managers or Russell 2000 index fund managers are trying to trade on this information, they may well not only contribute to the costs embedded in the construction of the index but also affect the ability of a good index fund manager to capture some of those embedded costs by trading at a different time from the moment when the index change is actually implemented.

Another unanticipated feature of today's indexing is that a great deal of congestion has arisen from the use of just a few indexes. Again, this effect is most clearly illustrated by the S&P 500 and the Russell 2000.

Furthermore, in some cases, indexes have extraordinarily high license fees. I happen to be most familiar with exchange-traded funds (ETFs), and I can say with a great deal of confidence that the total index license fees for ETFs, which account for very few assets relative to indexed mutual funds, are higher than the total index license fees for mutual funds. The ETF index license fee total is more than $75 million a year and growing steadily. The license fees for ETFs are almost invariably a function of assets, whereas some mutual funds pay a flat fee. With the index license fees high and growing, many new index providers are getting into the business. The index publishing business is hard to enter in some respects, but once a firm is in and has a number of contracts, it can be a very lucrative business. It is certainly profitable for the major index providers.

A collateral concern about the embedded expenses in an index fund is: What happens if the return environment turns out to be lower than it has been historically? To the extent that managers need to get every basis point they can in terms of the management of their portfolios, they will need to focus on costs.

A final, unanticipated feature that is making traditional indexing passé is that a lot of special purpose baskets are available that are called index funds. These funds are index funds primarily because of the regulatory environment within which they operate. They are not really index funds, at least not in terms of what the pioneers of indexing were describing.

Addressing Some of the Problems

The problems with indexing are not insurmountable. In this section, I will look at various ways to handle some of these problems.

Silent Indexes. One solution to several of the problems with traditional indexing is to have silent indexes. Silent indexing is a very simple concept. A silent index eliminates the transaction-cost impact that is embedded in indexes because of the preannouncement of index changes. A firm can have an objective process for creating or changing the composition of an index, but it does not have to announce what that process is to the public. The firm can say: "We have a broad market index fund" or "We have a growth fund or style fund, and it is an index fund." The firm can have its process and announce the changes after they are made in the fund, but it does not have to announce them in advance. Most S&P 500 capitalization range index funds could add 25–50 bps a year by being silent index funds, and a Russell 2000–type fund could add as much as a couple of hundred basis points. Some of the style indexes may be able to add even more because they should be able to reduce their transaction costs sharply.

One drawback is that if index funds do become silent index funds, a new paradigm will be needed for marketing the funds. By and large, today's index funds are marketed as S&P, Russell, or Dow Jones index funds. If the underlying asset benchmark is silent (i.e., unknown), they could no longer be marketed as such. Endorsement by major institutional indexers of the silent indexing approach could provide the marketing help—with benefits for all parties.

Buffer Zones. A partial solution to turnover and transaction costs is to use buffer zones on some funds. Buffer zones can be well constructed or poorly constructed. What I am suggesting is buffer zones to delay the process by which turnover in index funds occurs. A buffer zone between the Russell 1000 Index and the Russell 2000 might work well, but it would only work in the long run if the size of the money indexed to the two indexes is appropriate given the relative size of the stock universes represented by the funds. In other words, the amount of money indexed to the Russell 1000 would have to be a great deal larger than it is today to avoid the fire drill atmosphere that occurs every June when the Russell 2000 is rebalanced. Creating good buffer zones is difficult to accomplish, but they are needed.

Weighting. In the article that launched this conference, Peter Bernstein correctly pointed out that one will get more of the benefits of diversification by using weighting schemes other than capitalization weighting for a portfolio.[5] Possible solutions might be to have a series of tiered weights or to have a consistent percentage of capitalization weight on the larger positions in the portfolio.

[5]See Peter L. Bernstein, "Points of Inflection: Investment Management Tomorrow," *Financial Analysts Journal* (July/August 2003):18–23.

Certainly, the weighting scheme must be carefully developed. For example, equal weighting is not likely to be a good solution for a frequently rebalanced portfolio because of the transaction costs it generates. In *Capital Ideas*, Peter Bernstein pointed out some of the problems with the first index fund, the Samsonite Fund, which used an equal-dollar-weighted index based on the NYSE composite; Peter described it in *Capital Ideas* as the "Samsonite nightmare."

Liability Benchmarks. One possibility that is at the core of the issues raised at this conference and that addresses several of the problems of traditional indexing is to abandon asset benchmark indexes at the aggregate policy level. Ultimately, an investor needs to measure asset performance against a liability index. A lot of articles have been published on this topic over the years, but by and large, liability indexes have not been used very much. Few actual portfolios focus on anything other than asset benchmarks. Asset benchmarks tend to be reflected in the policy mix, but abandoning asset benchmark indexes is the only way to eliminate closet (asset) indexing and may help eliminate congestion and front running. The downside of this change of focus is that managers will have to increase their understanding of transaction costs, and it is hard to imagine all (or most) managers operating with liability benchmarks without a lengthy transition.

Even if a liability benchmark is used, everyone will not be able to create a portfolio that gets them to the point where aggregate asset returns match aggregate liability returns. Ronald Ryan and Frank Fabozzi wrote an article in the *Journal of Portfolio Management* a few years ago that covered some of the same issues.[6] These points are also reflected in **Table 1**. As this table shows, no real correlation exists between asset and liability returns. In fact, the signs were different in five out of the eight years reflected in the table, and of course, the differences are frequently great. Thus, the problem with switching to a liability index is that the asset returns do not match the liability returns, and not everyone will be able to make them match.

[6] Ronald J. Ryan and Frank J. Fabozzi, "Rethinking Pension Liabilities and Asset Allocation," *Journal of Portfolio Management* (Summer 2002):7–15.

Adding Value through "Active" Management. Index managers can count on adding value in several ways. First of all, the "chimpanzees" need to be replaced. One of the standing jokes of the investment management industry is that even a chimpanzee could run an index fund. Unfortunately, a few index funds do perform as if chimpanzees were running them. What is needed are astute managers who understand the basic principles of how to add value to an index fund by trading at a time that is different from the time the benchmark index is changed to cut down on transaction costs. Managers can also add value by trying to cut down index license fees and by re-evaluating diversification costs and benefits. If investors accept the principle that it is OK to deviate from the benchmark index, managers could add even more value. Greg Sharenow, Melanie Petsch, and Steve Strongin have written an excellent article that discusses the way an enhanced index manager can add value to the extent that the manager needs to stay close to a benchmark; the article has some useful suggestions.[7]

In line with some of Peter Bernstein's insights in his "Points of Inflection" article, I would like to focus on where a free-range portfolio manager can add value. **Figure 1** shows where a manager has the greatest opportunity to add value for various categories of asset allocation and security selection. Clearly, the right-hand side of the figure is where managers can obtain the greatest value added—security selection and, to a certain extent, sector bets.

Index-Based Lessons for Short Sellers

Short sellers should be aware of some index-based opportunities. For example, a lot of work has been done on the use of ETFs on the short side as a replacement for futures, particularly on transactions where

[7] Greg Sharenow, Melanie Petsch, and Steve Strongin, "Beating Benchmarks," *Journal of Portfolio Management* (Summer 2000):11–28.

Table 1. Ryan Labs Asset-Minus-Liability Returns, 1996–2003

Item	1996	1997	1998	1999	2000	2001	2002	2003
Assets	15.21	22.98	21.37	13.69	–2.50	–5.40	–11.41	20.04
Ryan Labs Liabilities	–3.70	19.63	16.23	–12.70	25.96	3.08	19.47	1.96
Assets – Liabilities	18.91	3.35	5.14	26.39	–28.46	–8.48	–30.88	18.08

Notes: Assets are 5 percent cash, 30 percent Lehman Brothers Aggregate Bond Index, 60 percent S&P 500, and 5 percent MSCI EAFE (Europe/Australasia/Far East) Index. Liabilities are equal-weighted Treasury strips (at one-year intervals).

Source: Based on data from Ryan Labs.

Figure 1. Percentile Performance over Horizon: Annualized Difference from Average, 1987–2001

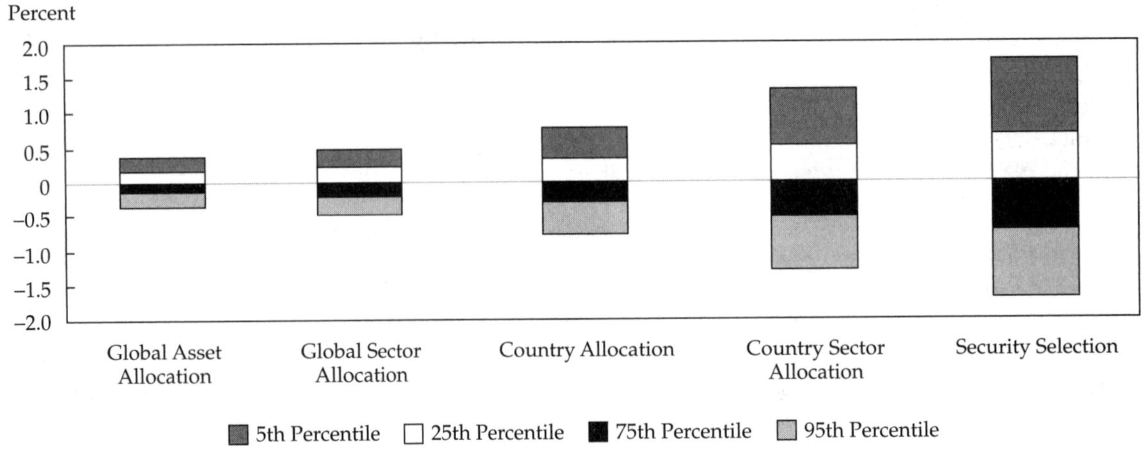

Percent

2.0
1.5
1.0
0.5
0
−0.5
−1.0
−1.5
−2.0

Global Asset Allocation
Global Sector Allocation
Country Allocation
Country Sector Allocation
Security Selection

5th Percentile
25th Percentile
75th Percentile
95th Percentile

Source: Based on data from Mark Kritzman and Sebastian Page, "The Hierarchy of Investment Choice," *Journal of Portfolio Management* (Summer 2003):11–23.

the hedging position is going to be in place for a long period of time. Using ETFs in this manner saves rollover costs associated with futures contracts. A lot of broker/dealers and hedge funds use ETFs extensively in risk management applications.

Note that I am not suggesting that short ETF positions will replace futures anytime soon, certainly not in terms of turnover, but ETF short positions are continuing to grow in terms of the size of the "open interest." What many people do not know is that the size of the short interest in some ETFs is considerably greater than the short interest of a typical stock. The short interest of the average stock traded on the NYSE is about 2 percent of the capitalization of the stock. Clearly, there is a long way to go before managers run out of the ability to sell the average stock short. Investors are going to run out of capable short managers long before managers run out of the ability to borrow stock to sell short.

An interesting feature of ETFs is that the S&P 500 SPDR (SPY) and the NASDAQ 100 (QQQ) each have short interest greater in value than the short interest of any common stock listed on the NYSE or NASDAQ—four times greater, in fact. **Table 2** shows the relative size of some of the ETF short interests. In every case, the short interest grew dramatically from the end of 2002 to the end of 2003, and for the NASDAQ 100, it was 55 percent of the fund's capitalization in December 2003. The short interest in an ETF can easily grow larger than the short interest in a common stock for a lot of reasons. Nevertheless, plenty of opportunity still exists for additional ETF short selling for risk management purposes.

Table 2. Short Interest Percentage of the Five Largest ETFs, December 2002 and December 2003

ETF	December 2002	December 2003
NASDAQ 100	22.7%	55.2%
iShares Russell 2000	26.5	45.0
DJIA DIAMONDS	25.0	35.8
S&P 500 SPDR	14.8	33.7
S&P 400 MidCap SPDR	9.8	14.6

An important factor that needs to be investigated in assessing possible growth in short selling is market structure. My specialty is product design and market structure issues, and thus I find it very interesting to look at the securities lending market. As Owen Lamont has said, "the stock lending market . . . usually works very well, except when you want to use it, in which case it works terribly."[8] That is probably a fair assessment. If you are a retail investor, you are going to find it difficult to borrow shares unless you are trading 10,000–20,000 shares. The whole securities lending process probably needs to be moved from the custodians to the Depository Trust & Clearing Corporation (DTCC) or some other like organization. Lending securities, however, is a significant part of the revenue of many custodians, so if it were moved to the DTCC, one would need to evaluate what custodian charges would be in the new environment as well as how all the economic interests involved would be affected.

[8]Owen A. Lamont, "Go Down Fighting: Short Sellers vs. Firms," working paper, Graduate School of Business, University of Chicago, and National Bureau of Economic Research (9 January 2003):4.

Question and Answer Session

Gary L. Gastineau

Question: Could you comment briefly on the history and future of ETF options and how they affect managers?

Gastineau: I have thought for some time that ETF options are likely to prove far more interesting than options on indexes. The simple reason is that an ETF option will settle into a physical entity, something that has a changing market value. With an ETF option, you will not have a cash settlement that occurs at an arbitrary moment in time and that takes you out of the market at the time of the exercise. Cash settlements concentrate demand for liquidity and expose you to attempts at market manipulation at the moment of settlement. With an option on an ETF, if you exercise a call, you can continue to hold the ETF for a period of time. You do not have to close the position out or change your effective exposure to the market at a moment artificially determined in advance.

The volume of trading in the QQQ ETF options, consistently the most active options contract in the world, demonstrates the popularity of ETF options. There are no iShares S&P 500 ETF options or SPDR options because of an intellectual property claim that I personally think is doubtful. It seems to me that it should be possible to trade options on SPDRs under U.S. SEC rules that are in place. Standard & Poor's takes a somewhat different view, and nobody seems ready to take them on.

As far as managers of the ETF index funds are concerned, having options on the funds is not an issue; in fact, it is a positive development. Unlike most mutual fund managers, ETF managers are insulated from the process of expansion or reduction in the size of their funds. Their role as portfolio managers is confined largely to changes in the composition of the index portfolio. As far as investors are concerned, I think options on ETFs can be a useful tool.

Question: How do you reconcile silent index funds and nondisclosure of benchmarks with investors' legal and fiduciary rights of disclosure and information?

Gastineau: Most of the legal issues involve SEC regulation. If you are a shareholder in Fidelity's Magellan Fund, you have the right to know what is in the Magellan portfolio every six months—and soon that will be every three months—with a 60-day lag. If that is OK for active managers, I don't see why it shouldn't be OK for index funds, particularly when it is clear that announcing the change in the index or in the benchmark before the change is implemented in the fund acts against the interests of the shareholders of the fund.

Now, I'm not arguing that you can't compare a broad market index fund based on a silent index with the S&P 500 or any other benchmark. If the industry benchmark is the S&P 500, comparing a large-cap silent index fund's performance with the S&P is appropriate. What I'm arguing for is eliminating the benchmark indexes as templates from as many funds as possible.

Question: Do you really think the market can handle an increase in short strategies, especially for ETFs?

Gastineau: There are a couple of issues here. Actually, if you can borrow an ETF on the same basis that you can borrow a share, selling the ETF short is a good deal for the short seller. The performance of most ETFs lagged their index by significantly more than their expense ratio in 2003. So, if you're borrowing on the same terms that you borrow something else, you start off with a good short position on a relative-value basis.

I'm not suggesting that there is a great deal of money to be made in an absolute sense by going out and shorting ETFs. That's not the point. My point is that to the extent that you have a system for securities lending in place that accesses the securities on deposit with the DTCC, there is no realistic limit that could not be accommodated by the market. Whether a particular short is a good idea or a bad idea is up to the manager, but if shorting ETFs is something that people want to do, we should make it as attractive as possible from a cost perspective. These short positions are excellent risk management tools. With the short interest on the typical stock at 2 percent today, I think it is going to be a very long time before issues of short-selling capacity become a concern. The open-ended nature of ETFs makes short-selling capacity essentially unlimited.

Question: Have negative rebates made shorting expensive?

Gastineau: I would urge anyone who is interested in short selling to read Lamont's paper (cited previously), and there are a number of other papers that are cited in his bibliography. The economics of short selling is a fascinating issue.

Some negative rebates can run into rates of 100 or 200 percent annually. Obviously, they're not counting on you keeping that position out for a whole year at those rates, but large negative rebates can, in fact, occur. For most of the market, there is no significant premium to borrow shares. There is a general collateral rate, much like a general repurchase rate in the government bond market, where there is no extra rebate associated with the transaction. If you get into some of the small stocks where there is sometimes a considerable difference in viewpoint as to the value of the security—the short sellers believing it is a piece of junk or that it is being manipulated and the longs knowing that it is a piece of junk—that is where you get these large negative rebates. Negative rebates are found in a very small number of issues, although they cover a significantly larger part of the market in terms of the amount of short-selling activity.

Large lending premiums also tend to occur in situations where various activities designed to prevent short selling have helped cause the stock to rise, perhaps to an artificial level. That is something that a short seller has to recognize. Negative premiums are rare in ETF share lending unless you are a very small scale borrower. If the borrowing demand is large enough, dealers will create more ETF shares.

